FISCAL HEALTH, RETIREMENT WEALTH

Your Prescription for Income Generation, Tax Management, and Financial Peace of Mind

By Prashant R. Sabapathi

This booklet discusses general concepts for retirement planning and is not intended to provide tax or legal advice. Individuals are urged to consult with their tax and legal professionals regarding these issues.

The stories and characters in this book are fictional. Each story combines facts and circumstances redacted to highlight the subject matter of each chapter. Facts and circumstances are fictional and do not represent any one client in part or in whole. They are included as an educational tool. No story should be treated to apply to the reader's individual circumstances. Always consult with your advisor before taking any action.

Copyright © 2022 by Magellan Financial and Prashant R. Sabapathi. Co-authored and edited by Carol Jean Butler. All rights reserved. No part of this publication may be reproduced, distributed, or transmitted in any form or by any means, electronic or mechanical, including photocopying, recording, or by any information storage and retrieval system, without written permission of the publisher, except in the case of brief quotations embodied in critical reviews and certain other noncommercial uses permitted by copyright law.

Printed in the United States of America

Second Printing, 2022
First Printing, 2021

Cover and interior design by the Magellan Creative Team.

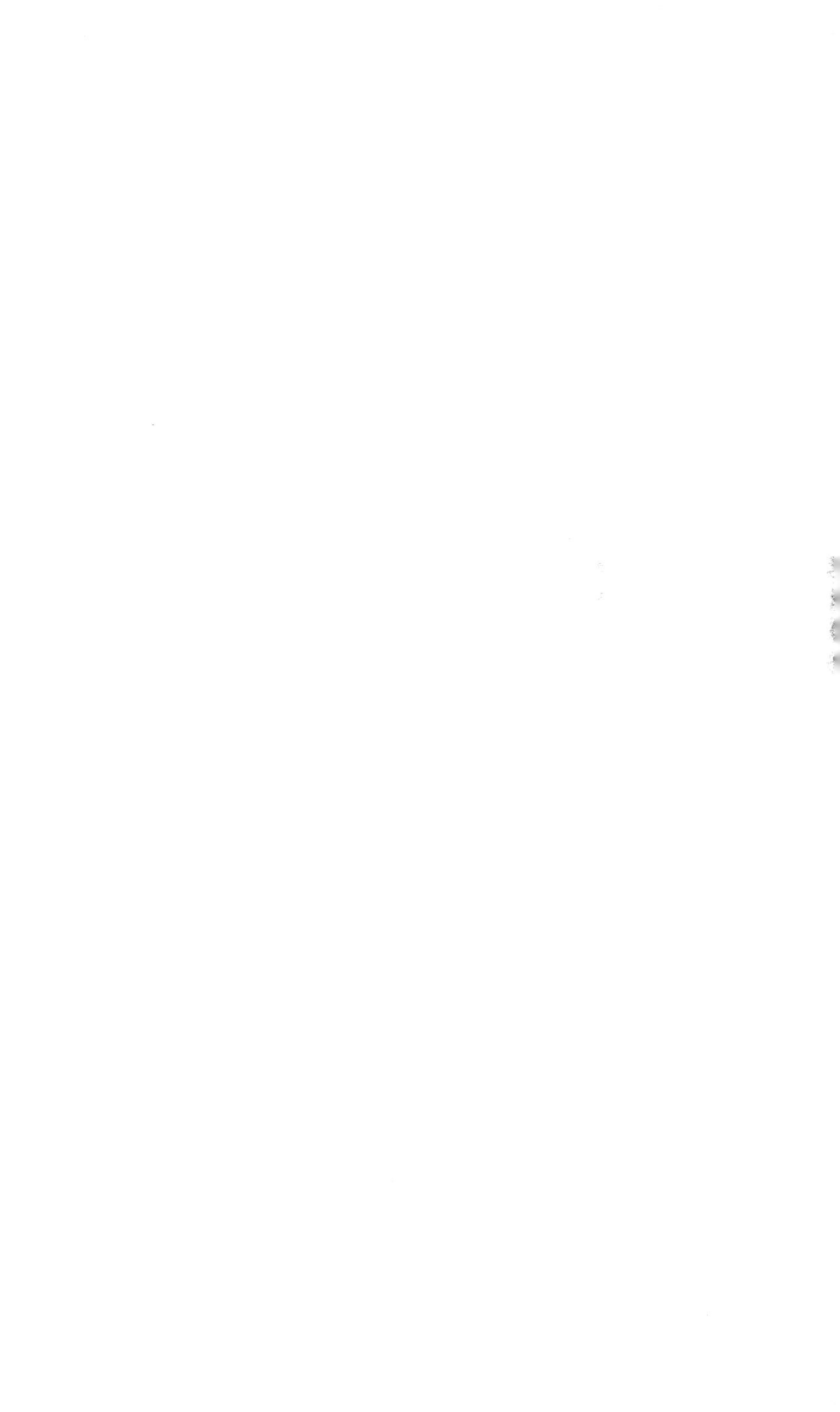

TABLE OF CONTENTS

INTRODUCTION: **THE HOLISTIC RETIREMENT** i

CHAPTER ONE: **GO BEYOND THE NUMBERS:**
YOUR RETIREMENT DREAM 1

CHAPTER TWO: **FACE THE BIG 5:**
DEADLY RISKS OF RETIRING TODAY 11

CHAPTER THREE: **FILL THE INCOME GAP:**
CHOOSE THE RIGHT STRATEGIES 23

CHAPTER FOUR: **OPTIMIZE YOUR SOCIAL SECURITY** 37

CHAPTER FIVE: **KEEP MORE OF YOUR INCOME:**
TAXES IN RETIREMENT 49

CHAPTER SIX: **RESCUE YOUR IRA:**
DESIGN A TAX-PREFERRED RETIREMENT 59

FINAL THOUGHTS 71

ABOUT THE AUTHOR 73

GLOSSARY OF TERMS 75

INTRODUCTION

THE HOLISTIC RETIREMENT

"It's not about running out of money; it's about running out of income."

During the last 50 years, we've seen a major shift in the foundation of the retirement structure. What once began with a gold watch and a cake and quite a bit of certainty now begins with market investments and the promise of volatility.

Most people back in 1950 received pensions at the end of their careers. They stopped working and knew that their paychecks would be replaced with a pension and Social Security. These two things covered their income needs; any savings left in the bank was like the cherry on top of the sundae.

Today, pension incomes represent a much smaller wedge of the income pie, and most people won't be receiving this slice of income at all. Most people have IRAs or 401(k)s where they try to save as much money as possible. These accounts are invested in the stock market with a focus on growth and return, and it's up to you to create an income stream with this money once you retire.

But how long will you need the income, and how do you make this money last? What can you do about rising taxes, market volatility, and the effect of global pandemics on the value of your retirement accounts? In short, how can you live your life during retirement with any degree of certainty during these wildly uncertain times?

My name is Prashant Sabapathi, and I come from a family of accomplished doctors. My brother is a doctor, both my parents are doctors, everyone in my family is a doctor—except for me.

I'm more concerned about your fiscal health. I can tell you that a lot of good advisors are like a lot of good doctors where they each have their area of specialty. Some doctors specialize in cardiology while others prefer pediatric care or oncology. And just as you wouldn't go to your pediatrician if you needed open heart-surgery, you also don't want to go into retirement working with the wrong advisor.

At this point in your life, you want to work with someone who specializes in the mechanics of giving you what you need: a comprehensive and coordinated retirement income. As an investment advisor representative held to the fiduciary standard of care, I can help you with all areas of your fiscal health, including taxes, Social Security optimization, and planning for long-term care. And because I'm an independent advisor, I have access to virtually every type of investment or financial tool you could need. To continue with our little analogy, you might even say I can write you prescriptions for both over-the-counter drugs and highly specialized medicine.

Whether you need aspirin or something stronger, I can get you what you need, but then I go one step beyond that and look at how these different financial issues interact. What are the side effects? How does waiting to file for Social Security affect your taxes, your RMD? What are the unintended tax consequences that can slowly but surely deplete your accounts?

It's only with this type of holistic planning that you can cure the worry and unease that comes from not knowing if you will run out of income. This book isn't here to give you Band-Aids; it's designed to help educate you about your choices so that you can take better care of yourself.

WHY I DO THIS

In 2015, my mother was diagnosed with dementia. She was only 57 years old and an accomplished medical professional. No one who knew her saw this coming, and it was a life-altering event, not just for my mother, but for our entire family.

Watching my father and our family go through this has reinforced the importance of what I do, and it's why I'm so serious and passionate today about a subject that many people find boring and tedious.

Over the last 40 years, defined-contribution plans such as the 401(k) have gradually replaced the defined-benefit pension plans as the primary retirement income vehicle, and this shift has *increased* the risks and responsibilities for anyone trying to manage their retirement today.[1] What is a 401(k)? It's not a promise of income that cannot be outlived once you stop working; it's not even a guarantee. It's a collection of investments that fluctuate and are dependent on market performance. Meanwhile, people are living longer, healthcare costs are rising, and taxes are taking an even bigger bite out of your Social Security income.

Retirement planning at its most basic level is about managing your cash flow versus your expenses. All that matters at the core, before we get into the weeds of investing, is this: how much money is coming in vs. how much is going out?

It's not about running out of money; it's about running out of income.

WHAT ARE YOU WILLING TO LOSE?

The way I solve this problem is through a risk-managed approach. I'm a big believer that *losses hurt more than gains help*. This subject, known as loss aversion theory, applies more specifically to someone who is in their 50s or already retired than it does for someone in their 20s or 30s. But losing

---

[1] Oakley, Diane, and Kenneally, Kelly, Retirement Insecurity 2019, National Institute on Retirement Security, March, 2019, https://www.nirsonline.org/wp-content/uploads/2019/02/OpinionResearch_final-1.pdf Accessed 10/11/2022.

during retirement isn't just about money. It's about freedom, independence, dignity, and the people you love.

Ask yourself, *what are you willing to lose?*

If the answer is nothing, if the people in your life and the dreams you've been nurturing are important to you, then you owe it to yourself to read this book so you can begin to write your own retirement prescription for success.

The study of holistic medicine was developed because the human body is made up of interdependent parts; if one part is not working properly, then all the other parts will be affected. This is also true for financial planning. If you have imbalances in your portfolio, if too much of your income is exposed to too much risk, if your taxes are not being efficiently managed or your Social Security benefits have not been coordinated, then that can negatively affect your overall fiscal health.

One can achieve optimal financial health—the primary goal of a prescription for success—by gaining proper portfolio balance. It is my directive to help you get a sound plan in place so that when contingencies such as coronavirus happen, you're not left dazed and confused. You'll know exactly how to handle it because it's already been accounted for in your retirement prescription for success.

Since 2012, I have been teaching classes and holding educational seminars, and I was recently named to the Council of Financial Educators (COFE). You can hear me as a guest contributor on the nationally syndicated *Financial Safari* radio show and see me as co-host on the *Retire Smart Maryland* television show. As a lifelong Marylander, I was also recently named to the Planned Giving Advisory Council for the Baltimore Symphony Orchestra. Since the age of four, I've been playing the piano, and from there I went on to learn violin, guitar, and mandolin. I can now play six instruments, which I do whenever things in my life get crazy.

As someone with a vested interest in the health and well-being of my community, I know that living well is about more than just money; it's about having a truly abundant life. As the co-founder and principal investment advisor of Elite Income Advisors, I am committed to helping successful business owners, professionals, and people like you accumulate, protect, and transfer their wealth while mitigating tax consequences.

It's never too late to get a start on the design and execution of your retirement prescription for success. I personally invite you to explore the pages of this book to learn how you can defeat the stress and achieve fiscal health to live the retirement dream you've worked so hard to achieve.

Here's to an abundant life.

~ *Prashant R. Sabapathi, Investment Adviser Representative and Co-founder of Elite Income Advisors, Inc., a Registered Investment Advisory firm.*

CHAPTER ONE

GO BEYOND THE NUMBERS: YOUR RETIREMENT DREAM

"You are never too old to set a new goal or dream a new dream."

~C.S. Lewis

The concept of retirement planning is for many people overwhelming. You might hear on the news, "You can't retire unless you have $2 million," and then go on to have sleepless nights. When can you retire? How much do you need? And can you afford to stay retired?

These are questions that need to be answered because retirement today has gotten more complicated than it used to be.

It used to be that just getting to retirement felt a little bit like winning the lottery. Only 56 percent of men made it to age 65 back in the 1950s, and the total number of Americans aged 65 or older was only 12.7 million.[1] You had no real dream for retirement because life during your golden years just didn't last very long.

Compare this to today, where at age 65, a man can realistically expect to live another 19.6 years and women another 21.[2] The number of Americans ages 65 and older is projected to nearly double from 52 million in 2018 to 95 million by 2060.[3] Most people

---

[1] Social Security History, Life Expectancy for Social Security, archival document, https://www.ssa.gov/history/lifeexpect.html Accessed 10/11/2022.
[2] National Center for Health Statistics, Older Person's Health, CDC, August 2021 https://www.cdc.gov/nchs/fastats/older-american-health.htm Accessed 10/11/2022.
[3] Population Reference Bureau, Fact Sheet: Aging in the United States, July 2019 https://www.prb.org/aging-unitedstates-fact-sheet/ Accessed 10/11/2022.

reading this book can expect their retirement to last anywhere from 20 to 30 years.

So, before we focus on your investments and the numbers, the first question to ask yourself is: What are you going to do with all this time?

> **Fast Fact:** More than half of all Americans are concerned that they won't be able to achieve a financially secure retirement and 67% say the nation faces a retirement crisis.[4]

STEP#1: DEVELOP A VISION

Television commercials, brochures, and promotional materials about investment products and retirement tools all have photos of people enjoying retirement. Walking along a beach or having dinner with friends are common scenes. But this is real life, not made-for-TV retirement. So, ask yourself, what do you want your retirement to look like?

Do you want to travel less or travel more? Downsize or maintain your current lifestyle? Spend all your money, live on the interest, or preserve a specific amount for a legacy?

Your retirement vision should be based on you, your family, and the things that you like to do, not someone else's definition of what the ideal retirement should look like. Not everyone wants to buzz around the country in an RV. So do a little digging and ask yourself some questions. Be as specific as possible with your answers. Don't just say, "I want to travel." Say, "I want to feel the water kiss my skin in the Seven Pools of Hana in Maui." Say, "I want to spend 30 hours a week in my studio painting." Say, "I want to play golf on every continent, in every state."

---

[4] Bond, Tyler et al, Retirement Insecurity 2021, National Institute on Retirement Security, February 2021, https://www.nirsonline.org/wp-content/uploads/2021/02/FINAL-Retirement-Insecurity-2021-.pdf Accessed 10/11/2022.

- When you close your eyes and picture yourself retired, where are you?
- Who are you with?
- What are doing?
- How will you spend your mornings?
- Your afternoons?
- What does your ideal evening look like?
- What is the one trip/experience/dream that your retirement will not feel complete without?

Studies find that living a meaningful life with a sense of purpose is fundamental to your well-being during retirement, and strong personal relationships and broader social engagement actually lead to better physical health.[5] After spending a lifetime developing an identity that is focused around career and means of income, retiring without developing a vision can be a shock to the system. It's never too late to identify the activities that give you a sense of worthwhile fulfillment, and the people whom you want to be spending time with.

Fast Fact: Studies consistently show that friendships are as important as family ties in predicting psychological well-being in adulthood and old age.[6]

STEP#2: CREATE A SPENDING PLAN

The first question people ask when thinking about retirement is, "Do I have enough to retire?" To answer this, don't use someone else's number. There is a simple way to figure this out for yourself: develop a spending plan to understand what you're

---

[5] Steptoe, Andrew, and Fancourt, Daisy, Leading a meaningful life at older ages and its relationship with social engagement, prosperity, health, biology, and time use, PNAS, January 2019 https://www.pnas.org/content/116/4/1207 Accessed 10/11/2022.
[6] Blieszner, Rosemary; Ogletree, Aaron M; Adams, Rebecca G, Friendship in Later Life: A Research Agenda, Oxford University Press, March 2019 https://www.ncbi.nlm.nih.gov/pmc/articles/PMC6441127/ 10/11/2022.

spending now. This includes digging deeper into your expenses by asking yourself which expenses are a *want* and which are a *need*?

The first 10 years of retirement are generally when you're going to feel the best, do the most, and possibly spend the most. So, we want to make sure you have what you need to be able to do what you *want*. Architects draft blueprints, pilots create flight plans, and writers develop book outlines. Financial advisors design spending plans.

Ideally, you want to track your spending for three to four months. Your spending categories—such as travel, fuel, groceries, clothing—can be broken down into two broader groupings: Needs and Wants.

Needs include the things required by the body for basic survival.
- Food
- Water
- Shelter
- Utilities
- Insurance
- Clothing
- Healthcare
- Medicine/prescriptions
- Transportation

Wants might be essential to the mind and spirit, but they are things the body could live without.
- Travel
- Vacations
- Hobbies
- Charitable donations
- Grandchildren spoiling
- New cars

- Dining out
- RV expenses

To develop a spending plan, look at what you are currently spending every month in the six areas of housing, healthcare, transportation, personal insurance, food, and miscellaneous expenses. Here is a breakdown of these six areas to give you an idea of what kinds of things you should include in each category.

Housing: includes mortgage cost, property taxes, homeowner's insurance, rent, utilities, repairs, maintenance, plus other fees and expenses.

Healthcare: includes medical services, medications, and supplies, plus health insurance.

Transportation: includes vehicle maintenance, fuel, auto insurance, public transportation, and rideshare expenses.

Personal Insurance: includes life insurance, umbrella policies, disability insurance, long-term care, final expenses, or any other insurance.

Food: includes both groceries and dining out.

Miscellaneous: includes outstanding loan payments, credit card payments, entertainment, travel and vacation, hobbies, gifts, education expenses, charitable donations, and any other expenses not listed.

As you start to record all the amounts in these six areas, you might find yourself thinking about how some of these expenses will change once you are retired. You might also realize that an item you thought was a *want* is really a *need*, meaning your retirement won't feel satisfying or meaningful without it. A true plan allows for flexibility and gives a way to finance both *needs* and *wants*.

Fast Fact: Most people can assume a retirement income replacement ratio of 80%, meaning they'll spend about 80% of the income they were making before retirement.[7]

STEP #3: IDENTIFY THE INCOME GAP

The **income gap** is the difference between your retirement living expenses and the income from guaranteed sources such as pensions or Social Security. You might also have other sources of guaranteed income such as rental income or a payment from an annuity.

Living expenses - guaranteed income = the income gap

Breaking down the income into two different types will help inform your decisions for funding the income gap.

To fund your income needs, consider using long-term, guaranteed sources of income that are not in the stock market such as annuities. This strategy will give you a sure thing. Even if a pandemic breaks out during the year that you retire and the market takes a 30 percent nosedive, the expenses you need to survive will still be covered.

To fund your income wants and outpace the long-term effects of inflation, consider using a combination of market investments such as stocks, mutual funds, exchange-traded funds, or managed money. This strategy will give you a maybe. During times of market turmoil, as long as your basic expenses are met, you should be able to leave these investments alone as part of your long-term growth strategy. When the market is up or the time is opportune, you may cash in these investments to fund one or more of your retirement dreams.

---

[7] Fidelity Viewpoints, "How Much Will You Spend in Retirement?" August 2021 https://www.fidelity.com/viewpoints/retirement/spending-in-retirement Accessed 10/11/2022.

Pat and Sam are wondering if they have enough money saved to retire. They know that their bills total $8,070 a month for an annual expense of $96,840. When they sit down and look closer at their needs vs. wants, they get a clearer picture: Their basic needs can be met with only $60,000 a year.

"But that doesn't include our trip to Australia," Sam notices.

"No, it does not," says their advisor. "So that's what we have to identify. How much of the $8,000 a month do you want to have as a sure thing, and how much are you comfortable with as a maybe?"

To answer that question, the advisor takes them through the income gap exercise. They discover that they will receive a total income of $32,000 from Social Security and another $25,000 annually from Pat's pension. This gave them a total of $57,000 in guaranteed retirement income.

They have no other sources of guaranteed income.

Doing the math, Pat and Sam calculated an income gap of $3,000 a year for their needs and a gap of $36,840 for their wants. This gave them a total gap of $39,840 annually.

"So, how much of this income gap do you want to fund as a sure thing and how much do you want to fund as a maybe?"

"Well, if we're talking about our trip to Australia," said Sam, "I won't feel like I'm living my dream retirement without it. So, I need that trip to be a sure thing."

Traveling to Australia for Sam was not a maybe. Sam needed to know that it would be a sure thing.

By getting clear about both their retirement vision and their spending, Pat and Sam are now able to choose their investments accordingly.[8]

---

[8] The above story is a fictional story using actual figures from sources believed to be reliable. This example is shown for illustrative purposes only. Estimated projections do not represent or guarantee the actual results of any transaction, and no representation is made that any transaction will, or is likely to, achieve results similar to those shown.

Fast Fact: Only 18% of Americans have a written financial plan for retirement.[9]

STEP #4: WORK WITH A FIDUCIARY

No advisor wants to look at someone and tell them that they can't afford to retire, yet that's why people seek counsel. It is an advisor's job to help steer their clients right, and sometimes that means telling someone what they *need* to hear rather than what they *want* to hear. But sometimes advisors experience what we in the industry call a *conflict of interest*.

The key thing to realize is that financial professionals go by many different names, and not all of them are held to the same standards of care. Sometimes because of where they work, an advisor will have an inherent conflict of interest when it comes to giving you advice. If they tell you, for example, that you're going to run out of money the way things currently stand, then you might make a change to your portfolio that affects their commission and causes them to lose money.

For this reason, you always want to work with a **fiduciary** *professional.*

Under a fiduciary duty of loyalty, an investment advisor must eliminate or disclose conflicts of interest which might cause the advisor—consciously or unconsciously—to give advice that is not in the best interest of you, the client. A fiduciary is also required to base their advice not on commissions from the product of the day but on the client's objectives.

This is why fiduciaries begin not with the numbers but with a series of questions designed *to get to know you*. Generally speaking, fiduciaries are more concerned with getting to know the person and establishing a relationship of trust rather than selling you a certain product or investment. Whether it's afternoons doing puzzles or river cruises in Europe, they will want to help you fund your dream retirement. And they'll help

---

[9] Fidelity Investments'® Retirement Mindset Study, 2019 https://www.fidelity.com/bin-public/060_www_fidelity_com/documents/fidelity/retirement-mindset-fact-sheet.pdf Accessed 10/11/2022.

you accomplish this in way that's in *your best interest*—meaning lower commissions, taxes, and fees.

> **Fast Fact**: The World Economic Fund reports that the average 65-year-old American will outlive their retirement savings within nine years.[10]

Prescription For Retirement Success: Having the right investments is only one small part of an overall retirement plan. To answer the question, *"when can I retire?"* first visualize your dreams, then analyze your income and expenses. Finally, identify your income gap. When choosing how to fill this gap, ask yourself how much of your income you *need* as a sure thing and how much you're comfortable with as a maybe. If the stock market crashes the month after you retire, you'll want to know that the health of your plan will stay strong.

CALL TO ACTION: How Do You Want to Retire?
- ✔ Figure out what you want your retirement to look like.
- ✔ Develop a spending plan.
- ✔ Identify your income gap.
- ✔ Work with a fiduciary to fill the income gap.

---

10 Wood, Johnny, Retirees will outlive their savings by a decade, World Economic Forum, June 2019, https://www.weforum.org/agenda/2019/06/retirees-will-outlive-their-savings-by-a-decade/ Accessed 10/11/2022.

CHAPTER TWO

FACE THE BIG 5: DEADLY RISKS OF RETIRING TODAY

"Investment decisions are now focused on the value of the funds, the returns on investment they deliver, and how volatile those returns are. Yet the primary concern of the saver remains what it always has been: Will I have sufficient income in retirement to live comfortably?"

~ Robert C. Merton

The leading cause of death in the United States today is heart disease. Cancer is a close second, followed by COVID-19, accidents, stroke, and chronic respiratory diseases.[11] Most people understand the leading cause of death to retirement: *running out of money before running out of life.*

Protecting yourself against this threat requires looking at your investments not in terms of the returns they earn but in terms of the income they can produce. Market risk is a concern, but it isn't even close to the number one risk that retirees face today. There are a lot more threats to consider and gaining protection from them is not as simple as taking a magic pill. As economist Robert Merton wrote in his paper for the Harvard Review, the seeds of the crisis in retirement planning lie in the fact that investment decisions are being made with "a misguided view of risk."[12] What follows are the big five risks to be aware of along with some strategies to address your concerns.

---

[11] National Center for Health Statistics, CDC, September 2022, https://www.cdc.gov/nchs/fastats/leading-causes-of-death.htm Accessed 10/11/2022.
[12] Merton, Robert C., The Crisis in Retirement Planning, Harvard Business Review, August 2014 https://hbr.org/2014/07/the-crisis-in-retirement-planning Accessed 10/12/2022.

Fast Fact: Higher unemployment in 2020, offset by the continued rise in stock and house prices, increased the National Retirement Risk Index to 51%.[13]

RISK #1: TAXES

During your working years, you're told not to worry about taxes during retirement. And we like that. Given the option to pay our taxes now or later, most people would rather pay them later.

That is exactly what happens if you save in a retirement account such as an IRA or 401(k) or Thrift Savings Plan (TSP), and the deal starts out as a pretty good one. The money comes out of your paycheck *before* this income is taxed, and it goes into your retirement account where it grows *without* being taxed, compounding interest. This allows you to accumulate a nice big pot of money.

Now, the closer you get to the time of retirement, the bigger that pot of money grows. For most people, their retirement account is the single largest monetary account they own. But whether you own a TSP, a 401(k), or a 403(b), what you have is a tax-deferred account.

The problem? You haven't paid any taxes on this money. Not on the amount you initially put in, and not on the growth.

Unless your money sits inside a **Roth IRA**, *you still owe income taxes on every penny you have saved*. That means Uncle Sam will be getting a certain percentage of your retirement account.

But wait—it gets even worse. He also has rules about when and how much money you must take out and failing to follow these rules will cost you even more in penalties and fees. This is why some experts call the money sitting in these accounts a *ticking tax time bomb*—whenever you go to spend this money, you never

---

[13] Munnell, Alicia H. et al, The National Retirement Risk Index: An Update from the 2019 SCF, Center for Retirement Research at Boston College, January 2021 https://crr.bc.edu/briefs/the-national-retirement-risk-index-an-update-from-the-2019-scf/ Accessed 10/11/2022.

know what unintended side effects might be triggered and how much your tax bill will explode.

Withdrawals from these accounts can increase your income, your marginal tax rate, the amount of tax you pay on your Social Security income, and the amount you pay in Medicare premiums. One withdrawal can have a domino effect, resulting in more of your money falling away. While you have zero control over tax law and Uncle Sam's rules, you do have 100 percent control over what you do with this money. That is the difference between planning for vs. paying your taxes, and we will be talking more about this in Chapters Five and Six.

Fast Fact: As of June 30, 2022, Americans own an estimated $33.7 trillion in untaxed retirement assets.[14]

RISK#2: LONGEVITY RISK

We've already discussed how people are living longer, spending more time than ever before in retirement. Obviously, this stresses your portfolio. Longevity is the risk that magnifies all other risks. Whatever is weak in your plan will get severely tested the longer you live. One area, in particular, has to do with the rising cost of healthcare and the type of services you may need later in life as your body ages.

It's long been reported that more than half of all 65-year-olds will require some form of long-term care (LTC), but LTC is often misunderstood. Long-term care refers to a wide range of services that you might need as you age, and these services could be performed in an assisted living center, an adult day care facility, a nursing home, or in the comfort of your own home. Services include simple custodial duties such as meal preparation or taking out the garbage to more intrinsic nursing care or twenty-fourhour supervision.

---

14 Investment Company Institute, Release: Quarterly Retirement market Data, September 2022, https://www.ici.org/statistical-report/ret_22_q2 Accessed 10/11/2021.

- 48 percent of people turning age 65 will need some form of paid LTC services during their lifetime.[15]
- 24 percent of people turning 65 will require paid LTC for *more than two years*.[16]
- 15 percent of people turning age 65 will spend more than 2 years in a nursing home.[17]
- Men will need LTC for an average of 2.2 years.[18]
- Women will need LTC for an average of 3.7 years.[19]
- The 2021 national average for the cost of a private room in a nursing home is $108,405 annually.[20]

Paying for these expenses is not only unpleasant to think about, it's a complicated problem to solve. Insurance companies have been rapidly exiting the long-term care market because of rising claims, low mortality rates, and higher prices in coverage than what most people can afford. At the same time, innovative solutions are being offered using other policy options.

This is an area of planning that became personal for me when my mother was diagnosed with dementia. She was the last person in the world who I thought this could happen to, and so I no longer believe it's okay to avoid this planning and think, "This won't happen to me."

When a long-term care event happens, it happens not just to one individual but to the whole family. And this isn't just a financial issue; it's an emotional one. We have little control over when or if these events will happen, but anything we do now to make the money side of things worry-free will allow you to focus all of your efforts and attention on where it should be—taking care of that individual in the way they deserve.

---

15 Benz, Christine, 100 Must-Know Statistics About Long-Term Care: Pandemic Edition, Morningstar, December 2020 https://www.morningstar.com/articles/1013929/100-must-know-statistics-about-long-term-care-pandemic-edition Accessed 10/11/2022.
16 Ibid.
17 Ibid.
18 Ibid.
19 Ibid.
20 Genworth, Key Cost of Care Findings, 2020, page 1, https://www.genworth.com/aging-and-you/finances/cost-of-care.html Accessed 11/03/2021.

Fast Fact: One out of every three seniors die from Alzheimer's or dementia, and in 2021 it cost the nation $355 billion.[21]

RISK #3: DEATH OF A SPOUSE

This is a risk specific to married couples or anyone cohabitating with someone they love. It's a common misconception to think that after your partner dies all your expenses suddenly get cut in half. Sorry, but that's not what happens. Your homeowner taxes, insurance, and mortgage expenses still need to be paid. Even if your house is paid off, the taxes and insurance do not get cut in half.

Most people in this situation find that the cost to maintain their lifestyle stays relatively the same, yet studies find that widows experience an income reduction of 35 to 40 percent upon their spouse's death. [22]

Here's why:

When your spouse or partner passes away, your household automatically loses at minimum one source of guaranteed lifetime income—Social Security. You might also lose pension income unless that person did some planning. Losing these guaranteed income checks creates a huge income gap that somehow needs to be made up.

One solution can be to optimize your Social Security benefit. The longer you wait to file for your benefit, the larger the income benefit grows. A strategy helpful to married couples is to allow the larger of the two benefit checks to grow as big as possible. Then, when one spouse passes away, the surviving spouse is able to claim the larger of the two checks under the guidelines stipulated for survivor benefits. (See Survivor Benefits in Chapter Four.)

---

[21] Alzheimer's Association, Facts, and Figures, 2021 https://www.alz.org/alzheimers-dementia/facts-figures Accessed 11/03/2021.
[22] Every CRS Report. "Congressional Research Service report: Social Security and Vulnerable Groups—Policy Options to Aid Widows." January 2020, R46182 CRS Report, https://www.everycrsreport.com/reports/R46182.html Accessed 10/11/2021.

Drew and Jordan had 100 percent of their $1 million retirement portfolio in market investments. They were relying on a low-cost buy-and-hold strategy with a certain percent in stocks and a certain percent in bonds.

They retired in 2008, and their portfolio lost 38 percent of its value. In 2009, it gained by 26 percent, but they were still not back to where they wanted to be.

They retired in 2010 with a portfolio value of $768,600. Now instead of feeling happy and excited about the years ahead, they were worried about how to fund their retirement dreams.[23]

Fast Fact: During the financial crisis that triggered the Great Recession, the S&P 500 index lost 53% of its value from October 2007 to February 2009, and it wasn't until six years later that the index returned to its pre-recession peak.[24]

RISK #4: MARKET RISK

Market risk is the risk of losing **principal** and interest due to a market correction. If that correction happens sometime during the 10 years before or after you retire, you might not have the time to make up for those losses. That could seriously compromise your portfolio's ability to generate income.

One myth commonly perpetuated by the industry is that "you can't miss the best days." A buy-and-hold strategy allows you to capture the full gains of the best days, but you also get the full losses of the worst days. Is this the best strategy to use for retirement accounts?

---

[23] The above story is a fictional story using actual figures from sources believed to be reliable. This example is shown for illustrative purposes only. Estimated projections do not represent or guarantee the actual results of any transaction, and no representation is made that any transaction will, or is likely to, achieve results similar to those shown.

[24] Parker, Kim, and Fry, Richard, More than half of U.S. households have some investment in the stock market, Pew Research Center March 2020 https://www.pewresearch.org/fact-tank/2020/03/25/more-than-half-of-u-s-households-have-some-investment-in-the-stock-market/ Accessed 10/11/2022.

I'm a big believer in the philosophy that **losses hurt more than gains help**. Let's put this to the test using historical numbers. From 1980 to 2015, the average return for the S&P 500 was 8.51 percent. If you had $100,000 in your typical buy-and-hold growth fund, and you missed the 30 best days, you would have received an average return of 3.64 percent. If you missed the 30 worst days, you would have earned an average return of 14.82 percent. Miss both the best and worst days, and you would have averaged a tidy 9.44 percent.[25]

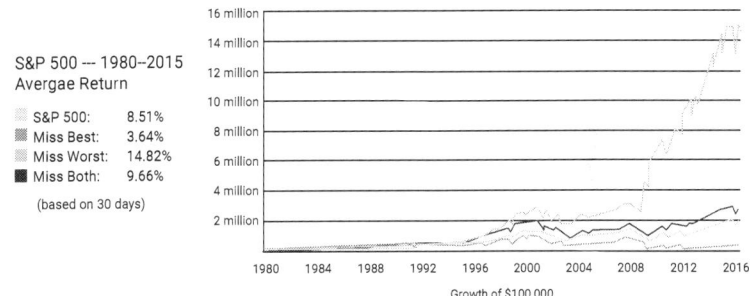

Source: Yahoo! Finance Annual Total Return (%) History.

If you want to remain in the market in the years just before and during retirement, it might be necessary to change your investment strategy. Ask yourself, how much could you lose before it made you extremely uncomfortable? Do you need this money to cover all or some of your income needs? How many years are you away from retirement? Do you have the time to recover from a market loss?

We will talk about your options for an investment and income strategy in Chapter Five, Filling the Income Gap.

---

25 Yahoo! Finance, SPDR S&P 500 ETF Trust (SPY) Annual total Return (%) History https://finance.yahoo.com/quote/SPY/performance/ Accessed 10/25/2022.

Fast Fact: Consumer prices were up 9.1% over the year as of June 2022, the largest increase in over 40 years.[26]

RISK #5: INFLATION

Most people understand the basic principle of **inflation**: the cost of things you buy will rise. A gallon of milk today will not cost the same as a gallon of milk tomorrow. The long-term U.S. inflation rate as of 2020 is 3.10 percent, which means prices will double every 20 years.[27]

Over the 12 months ending in June 2022, the Consumer Price Index for American consumers increased 9.1 percent, the largest 12-month increase since the 12-month period ending November 1981.[28] Energy prices rose by 41.6 percent; food at home rose 12.2 percent. The price of gas? That saw a 60.2 percent increase over this same time span.[29]

The year 2013 marked the 100th anniversary of the Consumer Price Index—the index that measures the change in prices. To commemorate the anniversary, the Bureau of Labor Statistics revealed its cumulative data in the following chart to give you an idea of inflation's curve over a 30-year period. The line on the top represents the increase in the cost of medical care.

---

26 U.S. Bureau of Labor Statistics, TED: The Economics Daily, July, 2022, https://www.bls.gov/opub/ted/2022/consumer-prices-up-9-1-percent-over-the-year-ended-june-2022-largest-increase-in-40-years.htm#:~:text=Consumer%20prices%20up%209.1%20percent,U.S.%20Bureau%20of%20Labor%20Statistics&text=The%20.,gov%20means%20it's%20official. Accessed 10/11/2022.
27 McMahon, Tim, Long Term U.S. Inflation, InflationData.com, updated Dec. 2020, https://inflationdata.com/Inflation/Inflation_Rate/Long_Term_Inflation.asp Accessed 10/25/2022.
28 U.S. Bureau of Labor Statistics, TED: The Economics Daily, July, 2022, https://www.bls.gov/opub/ted/2022/consumer-prices-up-9-1-percent-over-the-year-ended-june-2022-largest-increase-in-40-years.htm#:~:text=Consumer%20prices%20up%209.1%20percent,U.S.%20Bureau%20of%20Labor%20Statistics&text=The%20.,gov%20means%20it's%20official Accessed 10/11/2022.
29 Ibid.

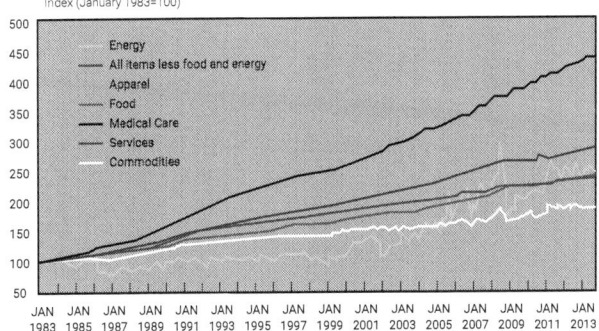

Source: U.S. Bureau of Labor Statistics.

One glance and it's clear: During retirement, it's not enough just to grow your money every year; **you also want to grow your income**. Your income should not be stagnant. It needs to increase each year just like prices increase each year and just like your Social Security benefit increases each year based on the consumer price index.

Prescription for Retirement Success: Solving the problem of risk during retirement involves choosing the right solutions at the right time so you don't get unintended side-effects such as a bigger tax bill or a smaller income. To further complicate things, the financial industry is one that is ever-evolving. Whatever the rules are governing products, solutions, and benefits today, you cannot be certain that those will be the same rules tomorrow. Tax brackets, income thresholds, and the age at which you must start taking your RMD have all changed in the last five years. Policies also change depending on the person in the White House. This means the time to take action against these risks is now before the current windows of opportunity close.

FISCAL HEALTH, RETIREMENT WEALTH   19

CALL TO ACTION: Know What You Own
- ✔ Make a list of your investment accounts.
- ✔ Identify whether they are invested in the stock market, bank products, or life insurance
- ✔ Identify what risks these financial tools are helping you to address: taxes, longevity, death of a spouse, market risk, or inflation.

CHAPTER THREE

FILL THE INCOME GAP: CHOOSE THE RIGHT STRATEGIES

"The question isn't at what age I want to retire, it's at what income."
~ George Foreman

Today's workers are relying on defined-contribution plans such as the 401(k) to generate an income during retirement. The challenge is that these defined-contribution plans aren't pensions or even a guaranteed place to put your money; they are places where you can invest.

If the goal of your investments during retirement is to generate an income, then you have to ask yourself how you are going to choose a strategy that can best help you do that?

You may have heard advice such as "live off the interest while preserving principal." But is it safe to stay in the market during today's times? The advent of the 401(k) resulted in millions of dollars being poured into market investments. Now, that money is coming out as the boomer generation retires. This makes the market more volatile than ever before. Combine that with our low interest-rate environment and the complexity of today's longer retirement, and you're tasked with a difficult responsibility: deciding how much pressure to put on your investment portfolio.

While every advisor has their own prescription when it comes to designing an income plan, some of the best strategies and income vehicles didn't even exist 50 years ago. This chapter is here to give you an educational overview of your options, along with a simple guideline to help you make your selections based on where you are today and where you want to be tomorrow.

Fast Fact: Only half of the workers surveyed by the Employee Benefit Research Institute said they were confident about how to withdraw income from their savings and investments.[30]

WHAT FINANCIAL PHASE ARE YOU IN?

Have you ever wondered why financial advice about saving for retirement varies so much from one advisor to another? This can make it difficult to know who to trust or what to believe.

One straightforward way you can wade through the riff-raff is to identify what financial phase you're in and then choose your investment strategy accordingly.

Broadly speaking, every investor who saves for retirement finds themselves going through two financial phases in their life. Those two phases are the **accumulation phase** and the **distribution phase**. What follows is the what, how, and who of the investment strategies you'll use during these phases and the kinds of professionals who can help guide you.

Accumulation Phase

WHAT: During your working years, you've been accumulating and growing your assets. In the business of financial planning, we call this your *accumulation phase*. If you're disciplined, or if you've had the foresight to set up automatic contributions, then you've probably gotten pretty good at accumulation.

HOW: This financial phase benefits from long-term *passive investment strategies* such as buy-and-hold and dollar-cost averaging. Basically, you keep putting away the money, and over time the money grows. Whether the stock market goes up, down,

---

[30] Greenwald, Lisa; Fronstin, Paul, The State of Employee Benefits: Findings From 2018, Health and Workplace Benefits Survey, EBRI, Jan 2019. https://www.ebri.org/pdf/surveys/rcs/2018/2018RCS_Report_V5MGAchecked.pdf Accessed 10/11/2022.

or sideways, as long as you don't touch this money, your account should move upward, which is exactly the outcome you want.

WHO: For this phase, it's common to work with a fund manager provided by the HR department of your employer, especially if you have a 401(k) or retirement plan with an employer match. You might also work with a stockbroker or a broker-dealer for help with the buying and selling of investments. You may even try doing this kind of investing by yourself using online financial services. You are, after all, responsible for making the lion's share of the contributions.

> **Fast Fact:** *Your choice of financial advisor can dramatically affect your retirement savings due to variations in fees, compensation, and conflicts of interest.*[31]

Distribution Phase

WHAT: During retirement, investors enter the *distribution phase*. This phase begins when you're no longer putting money into your portfolio or retirement accounts; instead, *you're taking the money out*. This fundamental shift changes everything you thought you knew about a sound investment strategy.

HOW: During this phase, investors are advised to make their allocation selections based on *preservation first* and *growth second*. Some advisors even usher their clients through a third phase, known as the *preservation phase*, five to 10 years prior to when their clients need this money for income. During the preservation phase, the portion of money required for your income needs is reallocated into financial instruments that better protect this money from market volatility.

However, given today's longer retirement and the likelihood of a long-term care event, most people can't afford to get out of the

---

[31] The Pew Charitable Trusts, Issue Brief: Choice of Financial Adviser Can Dramatically Affect Retirement Savings, July 2022 https://www.pewtrusts.org/en/research-and-analysis/issue-briefs/2022/07/choice-of-financial-adviser-can-dramatically-affect-retirement-savings Accessed 10/11/2022.

market altogether. They require some combination of short-term and long-term investing strategies and income planning tools that employ low to moderate risk.

WHO: To be successful during the distribution phase requires much more finesse and forethought than the strategies used during the accumulation phase. As we learned in the previous chapter, market risk isn't the only threat to your retirement portfolio. It can also be damaged by tax inefficiencies, long-term care catastrophes, and the problem of required distributions from tax-qualified retirement accounts. For this reason, you'll want to work with an advisor who specializes in this phase.

Just as you wouldn't go to a pediatrician when you need openheart surgery, you shouldn't go to an advisor who specializes in accumulation as you head into the distribution phase of retirement.

Distribution specialists are trained to ensure that your income lasts for the rest of your lifetime. They do this by coordinating your investment decisions with your distribution strategy for greater efficiency and healthier portfolio durability. They know how to look out for unintended side-effects such increased taxes or a hike in your Medicare premiums. They also know how to give you advice about claiming your Social Security. Ideally, these advisors are independent and able to give you access to a full spectrum of investments that include both securities and insurance tools.

- Insurance-only agents can get you access to income vehicles but not market investments.
- Broker-dealers can give you access to market investments but typically not insurance tools.
- Independent investment advisors who also have their insurance license—and most of them do—can give you access to a full spectrum of investments, including market securities, insurance tools, and actively managed investment strategies.

- An investment advisor representative is held to the fiduciary standard and legally required to give you advice that is in your best interest.

You might also want to inquire about the advisor's firm and the scope of its services. Can they give you access to a tax specialist? An attorney? Do they have a Medicare specialist on staff? Are they able to run a Social Security Timing Report to help you get a filing strategy?

In short, can your advisor get you the access you need to investments, strategies, and solutions specific to the financial phase you're in?

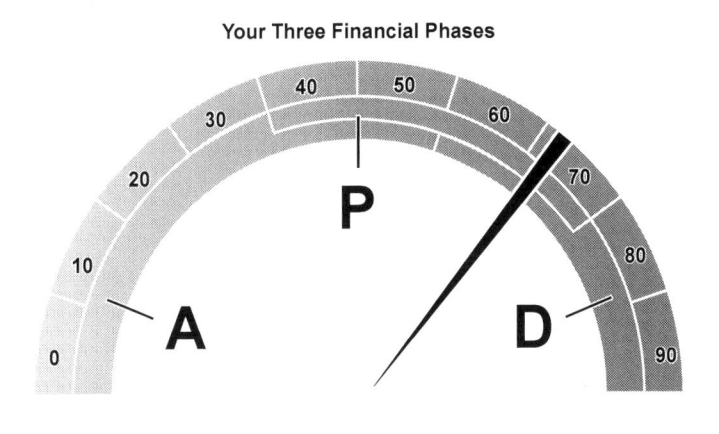

Your Three Financial Phases

A - Accumulation
20s, 30s, 40s, 50s, 60s

P - Preservation
40s, 50s, 60s, 70s

D - Distribution
60s, 70s, 80s, 90+

Source: Magellan Financial

3 WAYS TO GENERATE INCOME FROM YOUR INVESTMENTS

Because this financial phase is all about how to take the money *out* of the accounts, it's not just important to choose the right investments; it's also about timing. What the market happens to do during the years just before and after you retire can have a significant impact on how much you'll have left to fund your retirement income. For this reason, you may want to use a combination of strategies when filling the income gap.

#1 Using a Passive Investment Strategy

A passive investment strategy broadly refers to a **buy-and-hold strategy** with minimal trading in the stock market. Index investing is another common form of passive investing, where investors strive to replicate the returns of a broad market index such as the S&P 500 or the Dow Jones. The use of mutual funds is also common.

In order to be successful, this strategy requires a long time horizon of 10 years or more and a strong stomach committed to riding the market ups and downs. *While this strategy has the potential to earn the most, it also has the potential to lose the most.* The amount that you put into the investment is not guaranteed to be there when you need to take it out. This could make passive strategies problematic if you want a steady, reliable income.

There are withdrawal strategies designed to mitigate the risk, most notably the **4-percent rule**. This rule was designed to answer the question, *how much can you safely withdraw from your portfolio every year without going broke?* **While 4 percent annually was once thought to be safe with a failure rate of 6 percent, experts now find the projected failure rate for retirement accounts following this rule has jumped to 57 percent**.[32] The reason for this has to do with today's low-interest-rate environment and high market volatility.

Passive investment strategies may not be ideal for the person at or approaching retirement. While lowering the withdrawal rate to a more modest percentage is one solution, that doesn't satisfy the income needs of most people. You wouldn't take a pill if there was a 50/50 chance of death; you also shouldn't be willing to accept 50/50 odds when heading into retirement. Thankfully,

---

[32] Finke, Michael S.; Pfau, Wade D.; Blanchett, David, "The 4 Percent Rule is Not Safe in a Low-Yield World, Social Science Research Network, January 2013. https://papers.ssrn.com/sol3/papers.cfm?abstract_id=2201323 Accessed 10/11/2022.

you don't have to take this kind of gamble regarding your fiscal health. Today, better options exist.

> **Fast Fact:** The 4% rule for income withdrawal has now shriveled to only 2.4% for investors taking a moderate amount of risk in today's post-pandemic world.[33]

Rafe and Alex stayed in the market during the last 10 years and have an investment portfolio valued at $750,000. They are relying on the 4 percent rule to fill their income gap of $30,000 annually. Their broker set this up so the withdrawals are automatic. The same amount comes out of their account annually regardless of market performance, and the amount is adjusted annually for inflation.

Unfortunately, in the year they retired, the market fell by 20 percent. Their portfolio dropped to $600,000, and then out came their $30,000 income.

Year two of retirement, their account was valued at $570,000, and a 4 percent withdrawal would only give them $22,800 of income. Now they were withdrawing closer to 5.5 percent, but they weren't willing to take a pay cut.

Between February 19 and March 23, 2020, the market fell by 34 percent.[34] Rafe and Alex are realizing their withdrawal strategy isn't suited to the realities of today's times. Today, they need a better plan.[35]

#2 Using Income Vehicles

While the market gives us an opportunity to generate an increasing income, it can also put you at risk of receiving a decreasing income during market declines. One solution

---

33 Rusoff, Jane Wollman, "Wade Pfau: Pandemic Tears Up 4% Rule," Think Advisor, April 2020, https://www.thinkadvisor.com/2020/04/14/wade-pfau-virus-crisis-has-slashed-4-rule-nearly-in-half/ Accessed 10/11/2022.
34 Jason, Juli, "The Coronavirus Stock Market: A Market Gone Wild, Forbes, April 2020, https://www.forbes.com/sites/juliejason/2020/04/08/the-coronavirus-stock-market-a-market-gone-wild/#134b7b12a31f Accessed 3/2/2022.
35 The above story is a fictional story using actual figures from sources believed to be reliable. This example is shown for illustrative purposes only. Estimated projections do not represent or guarantee the actual results of any transaction, and no representation is made that any transaction will, or is likely to, achieve results similar to those shown.

designed specifically to give investors a certain income during uncertain times is income annuities.

An **income annuity** is a flexible insurance tool that uses an indexing method to give you market-linked gains without direct exposure to market risk. It has low to no fees, the money grows tax-deferred, and it passes to your beneficiaries without probate. The indexing method allows you to address inflation while receiving principal protection. The value of the account is guaranteed never to go down due to market loss, but the potential for market-linked returns is still there.

Income annuities can be very flexible. They can be used with or without an income rider to generate a steady or increasing income for someone in retirement. They can also be used as a savings vehicle for someone near retirement who wants to protect a portion of their funds. Certain types of income annuities have accumulation periods whereby the interest accumulates tax-deferred.

Because so many different types of annuities exist, be sure to talk to your advisor about the advantages and disadvantages. Typically speaking, these are long-term insurance tools with limited access to liquidity. **Guarantees are based on the claims-paying ability of the issuing company,** so shop around and compare different insurance companies to get the benefits and features best suited to your needs.

Fast Fact: Income annuities allow a retiree to spend at a level that investments alone would be unable to match without significant risk of running out of money before age 95.[36]

---

[36] Finke, Michael, and Pfau, Wade, New research from Principal shows annuities improve retirement outcomes, Principal National Life, April 2019. https://www.principal.com/about-us/news-room/news-releases/new-research-principal-shows-annuities-improve-retirement-outcomes Accessed 10/11/2022.

#3 Using An Active Investment Strategy

While a passive strategy operates under the assumption that you must stay in the market because you can't miss the best days, an active investment strategy operates under the assumption that losses hurt more than gains help. This is especially true for the investor with a shorter timeline.

The mathematical reality of account value restoration shows us that we can never get back to even by receiving a percentage gain equal to the percentage lost. For example, we often think that to recover from a 50 percent loss, we need a 50 percent return. In reality, we need an even greater return to recover from any loss, regardless of how big or small. Take a look at the following visual to understand why.

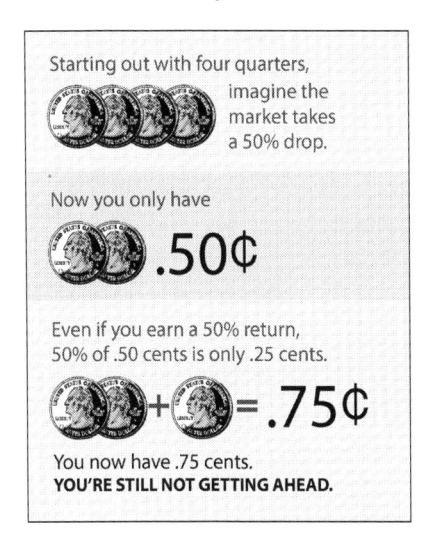

Starting out with four quarters, imagine the market takes a 50% drop.

Now you only have .50¢

Even if you earn a 50% return, 50% of .50 cents is only .25 cents.

+ = .75¢

You now have .75 cents.
YOU'RE STILL NOT GETTING AHEAD.

Source: Author's own illustration and not indicative of investment performance.

Once your account loses, the compounding muscle of your portfolio becomes crippled. You're no longer starting with the same base amount, and so it takes more investment energy to restore your account to its previous vigor. It also takes more time. It took over a decade for the average investor practicing buy-and-hold to get back to even after 2008.[37]

An **active strategy** seeks to limit loss through ongoing buying and selling. Holdings are actively adjusted based on market conditions and economic indicators. Instead of receiving 100 percent of both gains and losses, an active strategy limits loss in exchange for a limited portion of the gains. For example, an active strategy might seek to capture 70 percent of market gains and no more than 40 percent of market losses.

An active management strategy gives specified objectives tailored to the investor at or nearing retirement. If the market is heading south, your money manager has the ability to move your holdings to cash or other less-risky investments. This strategy comes with a management fee in exchange for a shorter timeline and the peace of mind you get, knowing someone actually is managing your money.

BEWARE: Many investors operate under the assumption that because they have a fund manager or pay fees to their broker, their money is being professionally managed. Unfortunately, this is not the case with your typical mutual fund manager. Specific language in the fund prospectus requires a fund to invest at least 80 percent of its assets in the type of investments implied by the fund name, a rule known as SEC rule 35d-1.[38]

This means that even if your broker or fund manager knows that the market is tanking, they can't do anything to help you.

---

[37] Roberts, Lance, After A Decade, Investors Are Finally Back to Even, Seeking Alpha, Feb. 2020. https://seekingalpha.com/article/4324760-after-decade-investors-are-finally-back-to-even Accessed 10/11/2022.
[38] U.S. Securities and Exchange Commission. Frequently Asked Questions about Rule 35d-1 (Investment Company Names) https://www.sec.gov/divisions/investment/guidance/rule35d-1faq.htm Accessed 10/11/2022.

Fast Fact: Research suggests that if you plan to travel and lead an active lifestyle, then you'll need to ratchet up your overall retirement budget by 6%.[39]

Miles and Mason decided they wanted to work with a fiduciary advisor. They knew they had to stay in the market to meet their income goals, but they were nearing the time of retirement. Working with a fiduciary, they designed an active management strategy for their $1 million portfolio that they both felt comfortable with.

Along came 2008. When the market fell by 38 percent, their portfolio only fell by 16 percent because it was being actively managed. In 2009, when the market recovered and went up by 26 percent, their portfolio gained by 18.2 percent.

Even after paying a 1.5 percent annual fee, Miles and Mason had a portfolio valued at $972,111 by the end of 2009. They were pleased with their investment strategy because everyone else they knew had lost by 30 or 40 percent. Moreover, for the next 10 years, they were able to take advantage of a record-breaking bull market run.[40]

Prescription for Retirement Success: Most people find a balanced approach between risk and safety necessary for the growth and protection they need to fund an income during retirement. When choosing from the menu of investment tools and strategies, be sure to keep in mind what financial phase you are in. An active strategy can be tailored to fund your income wants. By matching non-risk investments to your income needs, and risk investments with a longer timeline to your income wants, you'll stand to gain a greater probability of success during today's uncertain times.

---

39 Bond, Tyler, Doonan, Dan, and Kenneally, Kelly, Retirement Insecurity 2021, The National Institute on Retirement Security, Feb 2021, https://www.nirsonline.org/wp-content/uploads/2021/02/FINAL-Retirement-Insecurity-2021-.pdf Accessed 10/11/2022.
40 The above story is a fictional story using actual return figures for the years listed obtained from sources believed to be reliable. The results obtained are hypothetical and do not represent the investment of actual funds nor the performance of an actual account. Past performance is never indicative of future investment results. The performance presented does not reflect the application of all fees or trading costs.

CALL TO ACTION: Calculate Your Income Gap
- ✔ Put your income needs and wants into a quantifiable format.
- ✔ Identify all known sources of guaranteed income.
- ✔ Calculate your income gap.

CHAPTER FOUR

OPTIMIZE YOUR SOCIAL SECURITY

*"It ain't what you don't know that gets you into trouble.
It's what you know for sure that just ain't so."*
~ Mark Twain

There's a lot of things that people think are true that just aren't true. George Washington's teeth, for example, were not made of wood. They might have looked like wood, historians speculate, because his dentures became stained over time, but they were never crafted of wood.[41] Instead, our first president suffered painful contraptions made from ivory, gold, lead, and even human teeth—his own and those he purchased. By the time of his presidential inauguration in 1789, he only had one working tooth left in his mouth.[42]

Aside from inspiring you to floss more, this section is dedicated to giving you information about a subject you might think you already know a lot about: Social Security. It is the foundation of a solid income plan, comprising 50 percent or more of retirement income for older recipients.[43] This is an earned benefit you've paid into your entire working life, but how do you get the most out of it? Can you receive benefits even if you've never held a job? What happens if your spouse passes away? Can you work and collect Social Security at the same time?

---

41 Etter, William M, Wooden Teeth Myth, The Fred W. Smith National Library for George Washington at Mt. Vernon, https://www.mountvernon.org/library/digitalhistory/digital-encyclopedia/article/wooden-teeth-myth/ Accessed 10/12/2022.
42 Mount Vernon, The Trouble with Teeth, The Fred W. Smith National Library for George Washington at Mt. Vernon, https://www.mountvernon.org/george-washington/health/washingtons-teeth/ Accessed 10/12/2022.
43 Social Security Administration, Fact Sheet, 2022, https://www.ssa.gov/news/press/factsheets/basicfact-alt.pdf, Accessed 10/12/2022.

This chapter is here to give you some answers.

Fast Fact: Just over half–53%–of near retirees earned a D or lower on a quiz testing their knowledge about Social Security and basic program rules.[44]

FACTS ABOUT SOCIAL SECURITY: WHO, WHAT, WHEN, AND HOW

Nearly nine out of every ten American workers age 65 and older receive Social Security.[45] Known in its official capacity as *the retired worker benefit*, this is a lifetime benefit that pays out to a single individual every month for as long as that person lives. Who is eligible for this benefit, when should you file, and how much will you get? Welcome to the facts about Social Security.

WHO is eligible?

Anyone who works and pays Social Security taxes may become eligible for benefits by earning credits. The number of credits required to get retirement benefits depends on when you were born.

- If you were born in 1929 or later, you need 40 qualifying credits (QC) or 10 years of "substantial earnings".
- Work credits earned remain on your Social Security record.
- Benefit payments are based on the top 35 working years, adjusted for inflation using the Average Wage Index (AWI).
- If you stop working, then return to work later, you can add more credits to qualify.
- You can't receive retirement benefits on your record until you have completed the required number of credits.

There is another way you can still qualify for benefits even if you have not earned your 40 credits. Married individuals who never

---

[44] Franklin, Mary Beth, Third of near-retirees fail basic Social Security quiz, Investment News, April 2021 https://www.investmentnews.com/third-of-near-retirees-fail-basic-social-security-quiz-204852 Accessed 10/12/2022.
[45] Social Security Administration, Fact Sheet, 2022, https://www.ssa.gov/news/press/factsheets/basicfact-alt.pdf, Accessed 10/12/2022.

worked or have low earnings can get up to half of their spouse's benefit amount if they qualify. If you do have enough credits to qualify for both your own benefit and your spouse's benefit, the Social Security Administration always pays your own benefits first. If your spousal benefits are higher than your own, you'll get a combination of benefits equaling the higher spousal benefit.[46] Spousal benefits are just one type of family benefits eligible retired workers may receive.

- Spouses age 62 or older may get spousal benefits.
- Spouses younger than 62 may get benefits if they are taking care of a child younger than age 16 or disabled.
- Former spouses if they are age 62 or older may get divorce benefits, even if the former spouse has remarried, as long as they do not remarry.
- Widows and widowers may get survivor benefits as long as they haven't remarried before age 60 (age 50 if disabled).
- Disabled children, even if they are age 18 or older, may get benefits.
- Children up to age 18, or up to 19 if full-time students and not graduated from high school may get benefits.

WHAT is Social Security?

Social Security is a federal insurance program that provides benefits to retired people and to those who are employed or disabled. It is a pay-as-you-go system where taxes are paid into the program by working people to provide the benefits for the people who are not working. It's also a good deal: **Most people born between 1940 and 1999 who reach age 65 are scheduled to receive more in lifetime benefits than they contributed in taxes.**[47]

What the system is not: Social Security is NOT a system where you pay taxes into an account with your name on it so that

---

46 Social Security Administration, What is the eligibility for Social Security spouse's benefits and my own retirement benefits? October, 2022, https://faq.ssa.gov/en-us/Topic/article/KA-02011 Accessed 10/12/2022.
47 Steuerle, Eugene C; Cosic, Damir; Quakenbush, Caleb, How Do Lifetime Social Security Benefits and Taxes Differ by Earnings? Urban Institute, February 2019. https://www.urban.org/research/publication/how-do-lifetime-social-security-benefits-and-taxes-differ-earnings Accessed 10/12/2022.

when you retire, you can start pulling that money out. It's also not designed to replace 100 percent of your working income. The system was designed to give the average American worker insurance against the risk of living too long.

- In 1940, the life expectancy of a 65-year-old was almost 14 years; today it is over 20 years.[48]
- In 2022, an average of 66 million Americans per month will receive a Social Security benefit, totaling over one trillion dollars in benefits paid during the year.[49]
- The estimated average monthly Social Security benefit payable in June 2022 was $1,669 a month.[50]

Fast Facts: PIA is the primary insurance amount or the amount of money you're going to receive at full retirement age. FRA is the acronym for full retirement age. SSA is the acronym for the Social Security Administration. NRA is your normal retirement age, also known as your FRA.[51]

WHEN should I file?

The basics of getting an income strategy comes down to a question of *now* or *later*. The longer you wait, the bigger your check will get. **Delayed retirement credits** grow your payment at a rate of about 8 percent per year, which is a pretty good deal if you think about it from an investment standpoint. But there is a tradeoff: You won't receive a check during the years you wait.

Now: The earliest you can take your retirement benefit is age 62. This is known as filing early and it comes with a penalty that can reduce your check by as much as 25 percent. Each year, month, and day you wait to file reduces the penalty incrementally. **Full retirement age** (FRA) is somewhere between ages 65 and 67, depending on the year you were born, at which time you'll receive 100 percent of your earned benefits.

---

48 Social Security Administration, Fact Sheet, 2022, https://www.ssa.gov/news/press/factsheets/basicfact-alt.pdf, Accessed 10/12/2022.
49 Ibid.
50 Ibid.
51 Social Security Administration, Glossary of Social Security Terms, https://www.ssa.gov/agency/glossary/ Accessed 10/12/2022.

Later: The latest you should wait to file is age 70. Those delayed credits begin accumulating after FRA and they keep adding up to grow your payment. Age 70 is when the fruit is fully ripe and the benefit is ready to be picked. The following visual gives you an idea of how much you stand to gain or lose when deciding on now or later.

Projected Income Benefits Based on a $2,000 Primary Insurance Amount

AGE	BENEFIT%	BENEFIT $
Actuarial Reduction		
62	75.0%	$1,500
63	80.0%	$1,600
64	86.7%	$1,733
65	93.3%	$1,866
Full Retirement Age		
66	100%	$2,000
Delayed Retirement Credits		
67	108%	$2,160
68	116%	$2,320
69	124%	$2,480
70	132%	$2,640

Source: RetirementYou source materials © 2018-2019.

This is one decision where your personal health and relationships come into play. Married people especially will want to look at this decision from a two-person perspective. By waiting to file, your benefit will grow, and if you're married, this could result in a much bigger benefit check for your surviving spouse. **Once you file, however, you lock in the early-filing penalty for life.**

Fast Fact: 75% of near retirees incorrectly answered that if their spouse died, they would continue to receive both their own Social Security benefit and that of their deceased spouse.[52]

---

52 Franklin, Mary Beth, Third of near-retirees fail basic Social Security quiz, Investment News, April 2021 https://www.investmentnews.com/third-of-near-retirees-fail-basic-social-security-quiz-204852 Accessed 10/11/2022.

Deciding when to file for your benefit is also a retirement decision that could go on to impact every other aspect of your retirement plan. There are tax consequences, income thresholds to be aware of, and ways that your IRA income could affect how much in taxes you pay on your Social Security. While going directly to your Social Security office to get filing advice might seem like a good idea, employees are trained to maintain a neutral stance on claiming decisions—providing "information only" and not advice, noting that "there's no best age for everyone and ultimately it's your choice."[53] To help you choose, various entities from government agencies to for-profit companies have developed free, online benefit calculators and tools, but research has found that only 30 percent of the online tools succeeded in providing adequate advice while 70 percent provided inaccurate, ambiguous, or unclear advice.[54] For these reasons, a lot of people seek professional advice from advisors.

HOW much will I get?

Your **primary insurance amount** or PIA is Social Security lingo for the amount of money you're going to receive. It is based on four things:
- How long you worked.
- How much you made each year.
- The rate of inflation.
- The age at which you begin taking your benefit.

Because your benefits are funded by your wages, Social Security calculates an average of your 35 highest-earning years using an indexed system that brings your older earnings up to near-current wage levels. For example, the $13,587 salary you earned back in 1982 would be indexed by the system and converted

---

[53] Martin, Patricial P. and Kintzel, Dale, A Comparison of Free Online Tools for Individuals Deciding When to Claim Social Security Benefits, December 2016, SSA, https://www.ssa.gov/policy/docs/rsnotes/rsn2016-03.html Accessed 10/12/2022.
[54] Ibid.

into today's dollars for a salary valued at $52,014 for the worker retiring in 2022.[55]

And here's another bit of good news: Social Security also provides you with an increasing income to address inflation risk. Legislation enacted in 1973 gives a **cost-of-living adjustment** known as COLA to your benefit. This means **your payments are designed to keep pace with inflation.**

Based on the increase in the Consumer Price Index (CPI-W), the COLA for 2018 was 2.8 percent; the highest ever COLA was 14.3 percent in 1980; the COLA for 2022 is 5.9 percent.[56] Over the course of a 20-year retirement, these increases can really add up.

The more you earn during your working years, the higher your benefit will be, but there is a maximum amount of income that is taxable. This amount has changed over the years. For 2022, earnings over $147,000 may not be taxed by Social Security.[57] Because most people earn their highest salary during their later years, it's also important to know that working *while* receiving Social Security could cost you in taxes and penalties.

Fast Fact: *Average-income single adults retiring at age 65 in 2020 will receive more than $500,000 in benefits, and married couples will receive more than $1 million from Medicare and Social Security.[58]*

WORKING WHILE CLAIMING SOCIAL SECURITY

Yes, it's possible to legally collect Social Security even while you're still working, but you'll want to be aware of the rules. Keep in mind that any penalties that come out of your paycheck do

---

[55] Social Security Administration, Benefit Calculation Examples for Workers Retiring in 2022, Office of the Chief Actuary https://www.ssa.gov/oact/progdata/retirebenefit1.html Accessed 10/11/2022.
[56] Social Security Administration, Cost-of-Living Adjustment (COLA) Information for 2020, https://www.ssa.gov/cola/ Accessed 10/11/2022.
[57] Social Security Benefits Planner, Maximum Taxable Earnings, https://www.ssa.gov/planners/maxtax.html Accessed 10/11/2022.
[58] Kolasi, Erald, and Steuerle, Eugene C. Social Security & Medicare Lifetime Benefits and Taxes: 2020, Tax Policy Institute, November 2020, https://www.urban.org/sites/default/files/publication/103243/social-security-and-medicare-lifetime-benefits-and-taxes-2020_0.pdf Accessed 10/11/2022.

eventually make their way back to you. They will increase your benefits later, but by later, we're talking about 15 or so years. So, you might want to do some planning if you want to work while claiming, especially if you're married.

BEFORE FRA:

Between the ages of 62 and your FRA, if you are working and collecting Social Security, **every $1 of income that you earn over the threshold—which for 2022 is $19,560—will cost you a 50 percent penalty.**[59] Consider either working part-time to earn less than $19,560, or waiting to file for your benefit until after you reach full retirement age.

AFTER FRA:

The year you reach full retirement age, two things happen:

1. the SSA uses a different formula to assess the work penalty, and
2. it raises the income threshold.

The year you reach full retirement age, they will only deduct $1 for every $3 that you earn above the (higher) income limit, which for 2022 is $51,960.[60] Furthermore, they will only count the earnings you received before the month you reached full retirement age. In other words, after FRA, you can work as much as you want and still receive your Social Security benefit without penalty.

What about the year you retire? Good question. Most people will have earnings over the limit during that year, but don't worry!

There is a special rule that applies to earnings for the year that you retire. This rule says that if Social Security considers you retired, they will pay you a full Social Security check regardless of your income earnings from work.

---

[59] Social Security Administration, Benefits Planner: Retirement: Getting Benefits While Working https://www.ssa.gov/planners/retire/whileworking.html Accessed 10/11/2022.
[60] Ibid.

Fast Fact: Women make up 96% of Social Security survivor beneficiaries.[61]

ARE YOU ENTITLED TO SURVIVOR BENEFITS?

Spousal benefits—including divorce benefits—are Social Security benefits paid out to married individuals who may qualify even if they didn't work. Spousal benefits are based on a *living* spouse or ex-spouse's work history; survivor benefits are based on a *deceased* spouse or ex-spouse's work history.

Survivor benefits are a category of spousal benefits that pay out only after the death of a spouse. Also called widow or widower benefits, there are some seemingly perplexing rules about these benefits— when and how you file for them matters.

For example, you cannot file for survivor's benefits online, and you may not receive survivor benefits if you remarry before the age of 60.[62] You must also have been married for a minimum of nine months prior to the death of your spouse.

The survivor benefit is based on two things:

1. When the deceased filed.
2. When the survivor files.

When one spouse passes away, the survivor (given they meet all the requirements) has the option to receive the larger of two benefit amounts:

1. Their own benefit check.
2. The benefit check of the deceased.

For example, if your deceased spouse was receiving $3,000 a month, and you're only receiving $1,500 a month, you can apply

---

61 Center on Budget and Policy Priorities, Policy Basics: Top Ten Facts about Social Security, updated March 2022, ttps://www.cbpp.org/research/social-security/top-ten-facts-about-social-security Accessed 10/12/2022.
62 Social Security Administration, If You Are the Survivor, updated 2022, https://www.ssa.gov/benefits/survivors/ifyou.html#:~:text=If%20you%20remarry%20after%20you,1213%20to%20request%20an%20appointment Accessed 10/12/2022.

for survivor benefits and receive the $3,000 a month check instead.

With widow/widower benefits, it's also possible to allow your own benefit check to grow, gaining those delayed retirement credits while receiving a survivor benefit, and then switching over to your own benefit once you reach age 70.[63] The complexity of these rules means that you'll want to get professional advice before filing. Be sure that this person is qualified to give advice—millions of dollars are being left on the table due to improper filing strategies.

> **Fast Fact:** According to a SSA Office of the Inspector General report, 80% of widows and widowers eligible for survivor benefits could lose $530.9 million in benefits over their lifetimes due to incorrect filing.[64]

Divorce benefits might also be another category of survivor benefits, depending on how you felt about the marriage. To qualify, you and your spouse must have been married for at least 10 years and divorced for at least two years in cases where you haven't yet filed for benefits.[65] Divorce benefits apply to both the ex-wife and the ex-husband, and they also apply to couples in a same-sex marriage. Your ex has no say on whether or not you can file for divorce benefits and doing so will NOT reduce your exspouse's benefit, so talk to your advisor to find out if you qualify.

THE FUTURE OF SOCIAL SECURITY

We all know that the Social Security system is facing a future shortfall. The tsunami wave of boomers retiring combined with longer life expectancies means there's more money flowing out of

---

63 Ibid.
64 SSA, Office of the Inspector General Audit Report Summary, Retirement Beneficiaries Potentially Eligible for Widow(er)'s Benefits, June 2020, chrome-extension://efaidnbmnnnibpcajpcglclefindmkaj/https://oig-files.ssa.gov/audits/summary/A-13-13-23109Summary.pdf Accessed 10/12/2022.
65 Social Security Administration, Understanding Benefits, 2022 https://www.ssa.gov/pubs/EN-05-10024.pdf Accessed 3/02/2022.

the system than in. The number of Americans aged 65 and older will increase from about 58 million in 2022 to about 76 million by 2035.[66]

The system's trust funds were designed to bridge such gaps, but by tapping into that, the program based on current laws will only able to pay out 78 percent of benefits come 2034.[67]

There are several proposals to save Social Security. These proposals include increasing FRA for individuals born after 1960, decreasing the cost-of-living adjustments, changing the PIA benefit formula, reducing the delayed retirement credits, and increasing payroll taxes. Aside from casting your vote, you don't have any control over what does or doesn't change, but you can make sure you're receiving every dollar that you're entitled to.

Prescription for Retirement Success: The uncertainty of today's times puts even more pressure on the ability of your portfolio to perform. If you are at or near retirement, it's imperative that you test the efficiency of your plan against any unnecessary drains. This includes opportunities to optimize your Social Security benefit.

CALL TO ACTION: Optimize your Social Security benefit.
- ✔ Work with an advisor who is qualified and knowledgeable to get you a filing strategy.
- ✔ Ask for your customized Social Security timing report.

---

[66] Social Security Administration, Fact Sheet, 2022, https://www.ssa.gov/news/press/factsheets/basicfact-alt.pdf, Accessed 10/12/2022.
[67] Summary of the 2021 Annual Reports, Social Security Administration, Status of the Social Security and Medicare Programs, 2021, https://www.ssa.gov/oact/trsum/ Accessed 10/25/2021.

CHAPTER FIVE

KEEP MORE OF YOUR INCOME: TAXES IN RETIREMENT

"Today, it takes more brains and effort to make out the income-tax form than it does to make the income."
~ *Alfred E. Neuman*

We're all smart enough to know that mixing alcohol with certain medications is a bad idea. It can cause unintended side effects such as nausea, headaches, or fainting. That can put you at risk for internal bleeding, heart problems, or difficulty breathing. Furthermore, the side effects of these interactions are unpredictable and dependent on other factors such as your current health and diet.

The same kind of thing is also true for account withdrawals and taxes during retirement. For years you've been taught to save money in tax-deferred accounts. For years you've been accumulating wealth without paying taxes inside your 401(k) or IRA or TSP, and so the money just grows and grows.

The problem? **You're also growing your tax bill.**

Once you reach the age of 59 ½ and you're able to withdraw from these accounts without penalty, you will have to pay taxes. Even if you don't want to spend it, the IRS says you must once you reach a certain age. So, every time you spend this money you will have a tax event, and that can set off several unintended reactions such as a higher tax rate, less Social Security income, and a hike to your Medicare premiums.

We know that tax laws and rates change over time. *We know what the tax rates are now, but we don't know where they will be in the future.* All signs point to the probability of rising taxes. The more you can reduce your taxes, the less income your portfolio has to generate to support your lifestyle—meaning you can take less risk with the same outcome.

It doesn't take a whole of lot brains to look at your portfolio only in terms of the rate of return and how much it can *earn*. The real test is understanding the tax consequences of your withdrawals. This chapter is here to teach you how to think like a tax planner by looking at your portfolio in terms of **how much money you get to *keep*.**

Fast Fact: Studies find that a tax-efficient withdrawal strategy can help boost your nest egg anywhere from 1 to 11% when compared to conventional wisdom or non-customized strategies.[68]

TAX ME NOW, TAX ME LATER, TAX ME SOME, TAX ME NEVER

There are four types of money when it comes to your assets. And for the purposes of this chapter, we're including Social Security in the equation because it is arguably one of the biggest retirement assets that you own. It is also a tax-advantaged source of income.

One way to keep more of your income is to learn how to maximize the spending of tax-advantaged income while keeping below certain thresholds. Let's examine the four different kinds of money and the role each plays in determining your cash flow.

Taxable: You will pay taxes every year on the money inside taxable accounts. This income is reported as dividend or interest income on your 1099 tax form. Most people have at least some money in taxable accounts. Examples of these accounts include your savings, money market savings accounts, individual

---

[68] Geisler, Greg; Harden, Bill; Hulse, David S., A Comparison of the Tax Efficiency of Decumulation Strategies, Financial Planning Association (FPA), March 2021, https://www.financialplanningassociation.org/article/journal/MAR21-comparison-tax-efficiency-decumulation-strategies Accessed 10/12/2022.

bonds, individual stocks, and brokerage accounts that are not retirement accounts.

While long-term capital gains are considered taxable income, it is also an example of tax-advantaged income because these earnings are taxed at a lower rate than your regular income. Thanks to the 2017 increase in the standard deduction, some people don't have to pay taxes on their capital gains. If you have a lot of assets in taxable brokerage accounts, then you might want to work with a knowledgeable advisor to take advantage of untaxed capital gains to do tax planning rather than simply tax paying.

> **Fast Fact:** Income taxes can be the single largest expense for many retirees.[69]

Tax-deferred: Tax-deferred accounts are sometimes called qualified accounts. Why? Because they qualify for a certain kind of tax treatment. This deal allows you to save the money *before* the income has been taxed, allowing it to grow tax-deferred until you go to spend it *later*. If you're participating in your company's retirement plan such as a 401(k) or a Thrift Savings Plan, a 403(b), 457, IRA, SEP IRA, Simple IRA, Spousal IRA, or profit-sharing plans, then congratulations, you will qualify for retirement taxes.

These taxes come due when you take this money out. If you don't need the money right away and you want to keep growing it, you'll still be required to take it out later. The tax-deferred retirement accounts listed above all have **required minimum distributions**—known as the RMD—that become due once you reach a certain age.

If this account grows too large, future withdrawals (or even just your RMD obligations) could drive you into higher tax brackets, causing negative interactions with your Social Security income, your tax bill, and your Medicare premiums.

---

[69] FINRA, Taxation of Retirement Income, https://www.finra.org/investors/learn-to-invest/types-investments/retirement/managing-retirement-income/taxation-retirement-income#:~:text=You%20have%20to%20pay%20income,you%20have%20left%20to%20spend Accessed 2/23/2022.

> *Fast Fact:* Between the ages of 59½ and 72 (or for some people age 70½), there is no rule that restricts how much or how little you must take out of your tax-deferred retirement account.[70]

Tax-advantaged and tax-free: Tax-advantaged accounts give you tax-preferential treatment on your income while tax-free accounts give you tax-free income.

Everybody gets some form of tax-advantaged income during retirement thanks to Social Security. At least 15 percent of this income will be paid to you tax-free, and some people receive all of this income tax-free. How much of your Social Security income will be taxed depends on your *combined income*. Social Security income may also be taxed at the state level, depending on the state that you file your taxes in, and we will list those states later in this chapter.

All Roth IRA accounts will give you tax-free income. ***Every dollar you take out of a Roth will cost you zero dollars in taxes.*** With a Roth IRA, even the gains earned by the money comes to you tax-free, which is why many people consider doing a Roth conversion. Every dollar you convert from a **traditional IRA** into a Roth IRA will come back to you in the form of retirement income that is tax-free.

Here is the cliff-notes version of your tax landscape to make this easier to remember:

Taxable accounts = tax me now.
Tax-deferred accounts = tax me later.
Tax-advantaged = tax me some.
Tax-free accounts = tax me never.

HOW YOUR SOCIAL SECURITY BENEFIT IS TAXED

Learning how to optimize your Social Security benefit also plays a role in gaining a tax-efficient withdrawal strategy. Because the

---

[70] IRS, Retirement Topics — Required Minimum Distributions (RMDs), May 2021 https://www.irs.gov/retirement-plans/plan-participant-employee/retirement-topics-required-minimum-distributions-rmds Accessed 10/27/2021.

income thresholds haven't been changed since 1980, most people will be taxed on this benefit. But there are ways to minimize the side-effects, and with proper planning, it might even be possible to receive more of this income tax-free.

At least 15 percent and as much as 100 percent of your Social Security income can be received tax-free.

Up to 85 percent of your benefit may be taxed, and it will be taxed at your highest marginal income tax rate. Unfortunately, Taylor and Jordan didn't know this.

*Taylor and Jordan are retired with a **combined income** of $90,000 a year. Their income includes Taylor's pension of $40,000 a year, Jordan's RMD of $30,000 a year, and one-half of their combined Social Security benefits at $20,000.*

Taylor and Jordan's provisional income exceeds the $44,000 threshold, so 85 percent of their Social Security benefits are taxed at their highest marginal tax rate. Because they are in the 22 percent tax bracket, and 85 percent of their Social Security benefit is $34,000, they are paying $7,480 a year in taxes on their Social Security benefit.

However, there is an unintended side effect of this. Taylor and Jordan are receiving $7,480 less in income each year! To make up for this and so they can meet their expenses, Jordan withdraws more money from the IRA. At a 22 percent tax rate, they have to take out $9,589 to compensate for the taxation.

Had that $9,589 been allowed to stay in the IRA, it would have continued to grow tax-deferred. Every year as the cost-of-living adjustment goes up, they get an increased tax bill, requiring more and more money to come out of the IRA. Over time, this could easily amount to anywhere from $300,000 to $1 million in lost assets due to Social Security taxation.

Taylor and Jordan need a better plan.[71]

---

[71] The above story is a fictional story using actual figures from sources believed to be reliable. The results obtained are hypothetical and do not represent the investment of actual funds nor the performance of an actual account. Past performance is never indicative of future investment results. The performance presented does not reflect the application of all fees or trading costs.
  AARP, How is Social Security Taxed? Social Security Resource Center, December 2021, https://www.aarp.org/retirement/social-security/questions-answers/how-is-ss-taxed.html Accessed 4/4/2022.

Fast Fact: The Social Security Administration projects that 56% of Social Security recipients will owe income taxes on their benefits.[72]

The two things to know when determining how your benefit will be taxed are your *combined income* and your *income threshold*.

INCOME THRESHOLDS:

The Social Security Administration bases the amount of your taxation on income thresholds dependent on your filing status.. They are set by law and not adjusted annually.

- **If you file a federal tax return as an "individual"** *and your combined income is:*
  - less than $25,000, then you may pay zero taxes on your Social Security benefit.
  - between $25,000 and $34,000, then you may have to pay income tax on up to 50 percent of your benefits.
  - more than $34,000, then you may have to pay income tax on up to 85 percent of your benefits.
- **If you file a joint return**, and you and your spouse have a *combined income that is:*
  - less than $32,000, then you may pay zero taxes on your Social Security benefit.
  - between $32,000 and $44,000, then you may have to pay income tax on up to 50 percent of your benefits.
  - more than $44,000, then you may have to pay income tax on up to 85 percent of your benefits.
- **If you are married and file a separate tax return,** then you probably will pay taxes on your benefits.

---

[72] AARP, How is Social Security Taxed? Social Security Resource Center, December 2021, https://www.aarp.org/retirement/social-security/questions-answers/how-is-ss-taxed.html Accessed 4/4/2022.

COMBINED INCOME FORMULA

The magic formula for figuring your combined income is the total of three things:

3. **Your adjusted gross income.** This includes income from your job, rental income, royalties, interest, dividend payments, business income, alimony payments, pensions, and annuities. This does NOT include your Social Security income.
4. **Your non-taxable interest income.** This includes any sources of tax-free interest income such as tax-exempt bond funds and municipal bonds.
5. **Half of your Social Security income.** This is where you add your Social Security income, but only HALF of this income is counted. The formula looks like this:

Your adjusted gross income + any non-taxable interest income + ½ of your Social Security income

=

Your combined income

Another side-effect is the addition of taxes at the state level. There are a handful of states that tax your Social Security income, however, some of them make special provisions. For example, Missouri, West Virginia, and Vermont only tax benefits if your income exceeds certain (generous) thresholds, and Utah allows a tax credit for a portion of the benefits, beginning in 2021.

Your advisor should keep track of the changing rules for your state. For your 2022 tax return, the 12 states that tax Social Security income are, in alphabetical order: Colorado, Connecticut, Kansas, Minnesota, Missouri, Montana, Nebraska, New Mexico, Rhode Island, Utah, and Vermont.[73]

---

[73] Mengle, Rocky, and Block, Sandy, 12 States That Tax Social Security Benefits, Kiplinger, December 2021, https://www.kiplinger.com/retirement/social-security/603803/states-that-tax-social-security-benefits Accessed 1/4/2022.

Fast Fact: The maximum amount of earnings subject to Social Security withholding rose to 2.9% in 2021, while Social Security recipients received 5.9% more income in 2022.[74]

GET A WITHDRAWAL STRATEGY

Once you're retired and living off your benefits and the money in your various accounts, you could withdraw this money willy-nilly without giving a thought to taxes. But, assuming a 24 percent tax rate and a $1 million account, you don't really have $1 million to spend. In reality, you only have $760,000 or $680,000 or even $650,000 depending on your tax bracket because a certain percentage of every dollar belongs to Uncle Sam. And if history repeats itself and tax rates go up, you might even have less.

Conventional wisdom teaches you to spend the money in your tax-deferred account *later* to let it grow as big as possible. But doing this could cause unintended side effects and negative account interactions.

A better option is to get a tax-efficient withdrawal strategy. This may require going against conventional wisdom to diversify your portfolio from a tax standpoint. Planning strategists find that for most retirees, **a more tax-efficient withdrawal strategy is to spend tax-deferred accounts earlier rather than later to reduce your exposure to higher tax brackets in the future.** The optimal approach seems to be a preservation of tax-advantaged accounts with systematic spending of the tax-deferred accounts, using Roth conversions to take full advantage of your tax-bracket thresholds during the early years of retirement. When done correctly, this strategy will deliver more tax-free income later.

How much more income?

The Journal of Financial Planning finds that for most retirees, **a more tax-efficient withdrawal strategy can help boost your nest egg anywhere from 1 to 11 percent when compared to**

---

74 Ebeling, Ashlea, Social Security Taxes Will Increase 2.9%, While Benefits Will Rise 5.9% in 2022, Forbes, Oct 13, 2021 https://www.forbes.com/sites/ashleaebeling/2021/10/13/maximum-social-security-taxes-will-increase-29-while-benefits-will-rise-59-in-2022/ Accessed 10/27/2021.

conventional wisdom or non-customized strategies.[75] This can add years to the life of your portfolio relative to the strategy suggested by conventional wisdom. Imagine more years of income without having to assume more investment risk!

Prescription for Retirement Success: Conventional wisdom tells us to spend the money in our taxable accounts *first*, and our tax-deferred accounts *second*. Most people want to put off the odious task of paying taxes for as long as possible. Really, who can blame you?

Problem is, what this does to your portfolio in the long-term is far from beneficial. Those tax-deferred accounts keeping getting bigger and bigger. When that happens, unless you have a distribution specialist who is guiding you through these decisions, what you're creating is a tax-torpedo that could very well blow-up your retirement.

CALL TO ACTION: Get a tax-efficient withdrawal strategy

- ✔ Identify how much of your future retirement income is in tax-deferred accounts.
- ✔ Get a tax-efficient claiming strategy for your Social Security.
- ✔ Consider spending tax-deferred accounts earlier rather than later to reduce your exposure to higher tax brackets in the future.

---

75 Geisler, Greg; Harden, Bill; Hulse, David S., A Comparison of the Tax Efficiency of Decumulation Strategies, Financial Planning Association (FPA), March 2021, https://www.financialplanningassociation.org/article/journal/MAR21-comparison-tax-efficiency-decumulation-strategies Accessed 3/3/2022.

CHAPTER SIX

RESCUE YOUR IRA: DESIGN A TAX-PREFERRED RETIREMENT

"And in the end, it's not the years in your life that count. It's the life in your years."
~ Abraham Lincoln

Nobody wants to run out of money before they run out of life. This entire book has been dedicated to helping you make sure there's still plenty of juice left to keep your portfolio humming. But if you don't need your IRA money for income, then you might be tempted just to let it sit there and keep growing.

We've seen how the traditional strategy of spending your tax-deferred dollars last may not be a good approach. We've seen how the uncertainty of today's times—the rising market volatility, the changing tax landscape—all seem to conspire against how much money is yours to keep. This chapter will show you how to leverage today's tax laws to protect what for many is their biggest asset—their IRA—from being overtaxed.

It was Benjamin Franklin who once said, "Nothing is certain except death and taxes." You might extend this to say, "*increasing* taxes." This is especially true of your IRA. Even if you don't want to spend this money, even if you have plans to leave your IRA to your spouse or children or a charity, the rules for IRA distributions say you MUST withdraw this money.

When that happens, your income will increase. That will set off a string of unintended side effects, potentially raising your marginal tax rate, the taxes owed on your Social Security, and even the cost that you pay for Medicare Parts B and D.

There is good news, however. This is one area of your retirement plan where you *have more control than you think.*

Fast Fact: Studies find that 40% of wealthy households–defined as having a combined income from Social Security and savings of at least $3,000 a month–are at risk of not being able to maintain their lifestyle due to taxation.[76]

WHY TAXES ARE CURRENTLY ON SALE

Let's not confuse *paying* your taxes with *planning* for your taxes. Paying your taxes is what you do every year by the deadline of April 15. By then, it's usually too late to do anything but pay what you owe.

Planning for your taxes means looking ahead—sometimes as long as 10 years into the future—and using current tax law to reduce what you owe.

So, looking ahead, how many people think that tax rates will be going *down* during the next 15 years?

Nobody.

How many people think taxes will be going *up?* Everybody.

When you think about retirement spanning 20 to 30 years, and you look at where we are today as compared to where we've been, it becomes pretty obvious which direction we're headed.

On November 16, 2017, the House of Representatives passed the Tax Cuts and Jobs Act to reform the individual income tax codes. This act lowered tax rates on wages, investment, and business income, and it changed the standard deductions for millions of filers, nearly doubling the standard amount. But these individual income-tax changes are set to expire on December 31, 2025, when

---

[76] Chen, Anqi, and Munnell, Alicia H., How Much Taxes Will Retirees Owe On Their Retirement Income? Center for Retirement Research at Boston College, November 2020 https://crr.bc.edu/wp-content/uploads/2020/11/wp_2020-16..pdf Accessed 10/25/2021.

tax brackets will revert back to 2017 levels.[77] The 2017 levels are higher for five out of the seven income tax brackets, so **most taxpayers will see a tax hike** unless provisions are extended.[78]

The top marginal income tax rates from 1913 to 2018

Source: Urban-Brookings Tax Policy Center. Statistics. "Historical Individual Income Tax Parameters: 1913 to 2018."

What this means for you is that right now we have a window of opportunity where it's possible to do some real planning. Taxes are at historically low levels. They aren't going to stay this low forever.

The relief package passed during the coronavirus pandemic drove up U.S. debt to $25 trillion.[79] Even before the pandemic hit, our debt was high by historic standards with our gross debt exceeding the GDP by 104 percent.[80] The projected shortages to Social Security must also be addressed because the annual cost of the program exceeded the total income beginning in 2021.[81]

---

77 El-Sibaie, Amir, A Look Ahead at Expiring Tax Provisions, Tax Foundation, January 2018. https://tax-foundation.org/look-ahead-expiring-tax-provisions Accessed 10/25/2021.
78 Ibid.
79 Gramlich, John, Coronavirus downturn likely to add to high government debt in some countries, Pew Research Center, April 2020. https://www.pewresearch.org/fact-tank/2020/04/29/coronavirus-downturn-likely-to-add-to-high-government-debt-in-some-countries/ Accessed 10/25/2021.
80 Ibid.
81 Singletary, Michelle, Even before coronavirus, Social Security was staring at a shortfall, The Washington Post, May 2020 https://www.washingtonpost.com/business/2020/05/25/even-before-coronavirus-social-security-was-staring-shortfall/ Accessed 10/25/2021.

FISCAL HEALTH, RETIREMENT WEALTH

The trust fund alone can pay full benefits until 2034, at which point reserves will become depleted and continuing revenues would be enough to cover only 78 percent of the program's costs.[82]

Logically, there seems to be only one direction taxes could possibly go.

Fast Fact: The highest marginal tax rate for 2022 was at a historic low. The highest rate ever seen was 94% in 1944-1945. It remained in the 50 to 90% range until it went down to 38.50% in 1987.[83]

THE WHO, WHEN, AND WHAT OF THE RMD

Retirement accounts have rules about when and how much money you may put in. Some of these accounts also have rules about when and how much you must take out. The required minimum distribution (RMD) is the amount of money you are required to withdraw once you hit a certain age. What follows is the who, when, what, and why of the RMD.

WHO: Anyone who owns a retirement account such as a 401(k), TSP, or an IRA account that is not preceded by the word "Roth" may be required to take an RMD. This includes traditional IRAs and IRA-based plans such as SEPs, SARSEPs, and SIMPLE IRAs. It also may not apply to Roth or non-qualified accounts. It may also not apply if you are still contributing to your 401(k).

WHEN: When you reach age 72, your RMD comes due. The SECURE Act passed in 2019 changed the RMD requirements by extending the age from 70½ to 72. If you reached the age of 70½ in 2019 the prior rule applies, and you must take your first RMD by April 1, 2020. If you reach age 70½ in 2020 or later, you must take your first RMD by April 1 of the year after you reach 72.[84]

---

[82] Summary of the 2021 Annual Reports, Social Security Administration, Status of the Social Security and Medicare Programs, 2021, https://www.ssa.gov/oact/trsum/ Accessed 10/25/2021.
[83] Tax Policy Center, Historical Highest Marginal Income Tax Rates, Feb 2022 https://www.taxpolicycenter.org/statistics/historical-highest-marginal-income-tax-rates Accessed 10/12/2022.
[84] IRS, Retirement Plan, and IRA Required Minimum Distributions FAQs, June 2021 https://www.irs.gov/retirement-plans/retirement-plans-faqs-regarding-required-minimum-distributions Accessed 10/12/2022.

WHAT: To calculate the exact amount of your RMD, the IRS uses a division formula based on two things: 1) your account's fair market value (FMV) at the end of the preceding year, and 2) the number of years that you're expected to live. Your RMD amount is then calculated by dividing your account's FMV as of December 31 of last year by your life expectancy factor.

For example, if your account's fair market value at the end of the year was $500,000 and you're expected to live another 27.4 years, then your RMD would be $18,248 annually.

The IRS calculates your life expectancy by looking at the Uniform Lifetime Table. This table calculates the number of years that you have left to pay the taxes you owe on this amount of money. Because we're living longer, the IRS updated the tables with new rates going into effect beginning 2022. The longer you live, the shorter amount of time you have to pay the taxes owed, so the withdrawal rates (RMD%) increase as you age.

FOR USE BY IRA OWNERS IN 2022 AND BEYOND

Age	Life Expectancy Factor	RMD% Equivalent	Age	Life Expectancy Factor	RMD% Equivalent
72	27.4	3.65%	97	7.8	12.82%
73	26.5	3.77%	98	7.3	13.70%
74	25.5	3.92%	99	6.8	14.71%
75	24.6	4.07%	100	6.4	15.63%
76	23.7	4.22%	101	6	16.67%
77	22.9	4.37%	102	5.6	17.86%
78	22	4.55%	103	5.2	19.23%
79	21.1	4.74%	104	4.9	20.41%
80	20.2	4.95%	105	4.6	21.74%
81	19.4	5.15%	106	4.3	23.26%
82	18.5	5.41%	107	4.1	24.39%
83	17.7	5.65%	108	3.9	25.64%
84	16.8	5.95%	109	3.7	27.03%
85	16	6.25%	110	3.5	28.57%
86	15.2	6.58%	111	3.4	29.41%
87	14.4	6.94%	112	3.3	30.30%
88	13.7	7.30%	113	3.1	32.26%
89	12.9	7.75%	114	3	33.33%
90	12.2	8.20%	115	2.9	34.48%
91	11.5	8.70%	116	2.8	35.71%
92	10.8	9.26%	117	2.7	37.04%
93	10.1	9.90%	118	2.5	40.00%
94	9.5	10.53%	119	2.3	43.48%
95	8.9	11.24%	120	2	50.00%
96	8.4	11.90%			

Source: 2022 IRS Uniform Lifetime Table

WHY: Because retirement accounts are tax-deferred accounts, you deferred the taxes—meaning you didn't pay them yet. But perhaps the more important question to ask yourself is "why are we talking about this now?" We are devoting a chapter to this subject because when you do take this money out, it gets taxed as ordinary income. And that may cause a string of unintended side effects.

Taking an IRA distribution no matter how big or small will increase your annual income. This has the potential to set off the following:

- An increase to your marginal tax rate.
- An increase in the amount of overall income taxes you pay.
- An increase in the amount of your Social Security benefit that is taxable.
- An increase to your Medicare Parts B and D premiums.

RMD Q&A

How much will my taxes go up? Crossing over the threshold into a new marginal tax rate can increase your overall tax bill by as much as 84 percent under current law, or 67 percent using 2017 tax brackets.

Married Filing Jointly

	Old Law		Tax Cuts and Jobs Act	
10%	$0-$19,050	10%	$0-$19,050
15%	$19,050-$77,400	12%	$19,050-$77,400
25%	$77,400-$156,150	22%	$77,400-$165,000
28%	$156,150-$237,950	24%	$165,000-$315,000
33%	$237,950-$424,950	32%	$315,000-$400,000
35%	$424,950-$480,050	35%	$400,000-$600,000

67% Increase (first three brackets on Old Law side) → 84% Increase (first three brackets on Tax Cuts and Jobs Act side)

Source: Urban-Brookings Tax Policy Center. Recent History of the Tax Code, "How did the Tax Cuts and Jobs Act change personal taxes?"

What's the deal with Medicare Parts B and D? Once you become eligible for Medicare, you will pay a premium each month, automatically deducted from your Social Security. Most people pay the standard premium amount; however, if your modified adjusted gross income goes above a certain threshold—even if this is due to a one-time withdrawal—then you trigger an increase to your payment known as IRMAA (Income Related Monthly Adjustment Amount). This adjustment also means an increase in Medicare Part D.

One common trigger of IRMAA is the RMD, so make sure your advisor is aware of how much income you are required to pull out.

Can I take out my RMD early? Yes. You can take out your IRA money early before you turn age 72 and any time after you reach age 59½. You can also take MORE money out of your IRA than required by the RMD, but you can't take less. Failing to take out the full amount, or failing to withdraw the RMD by the deadline, will cost you a penalty tax of 50 percent.

Blake had $500,000 in his IRA when he retired at the age of 62. Because he worked for the federal government, he had a pension and an amount from Social Security. He planned to leave his IRA money to his spouse and family. He retired and continued to let it accumulate, leaving it in the stock market where, during the next 10 years, it grew to just over $1 million.

Blake was proud of doubling the IRA, but something else happened after 10 years—Blake turned 72. Now, he was required to start taking his RMD. When he withdrew the $39,000 required, this amount was reported to the IRS as income. That pushed him into a higher income-tax bracket, increasing his taxes by 84 percent. At the same time, he also owed more in taxes on his Social Security benefit—at the new higher rate.

Blake realized he created a tax nightmare. If he doubles his money again at the age of 82, his RMD could require that he withdraw 5.44 percent annually based on the current life expectancy table. That income would move him up again into an even higher tax bracket, potentially causing even more of his Social Security to be taxed, more of his pension to be taxed, and more of his IRA money to go to Uncle Sam.

This is not at all what Blake had in mind when he saved this money.[85]

[85] The above story is a fictional story using actual figures from sources believed to be reliable. This example is shown for illustrative purposes only. Estimated projections do not represent or guarantee the actual results of any transaction, and no representation is made that any transaction will, or is likely to, achieve results similar to those shown.

HOW TO GET RID OF YOUR RMD

The rule of 72 tells us how long it will take for your money to double given a fixed rate of interest. For example, if your account is making 6 percent with a balance of $1 million and you retire at age 60, then you're going to see that account double in 12 years. That means when you reach age 72, your RMD is going to be based on a $2 million account.

Now, take a look at the Uniform Life Expectancy table and notice how the number of years (the distribution period) keeps getting lower. As you get older and your IRA gets bigger, you'll be required to take out *more* money on a percentage basis from an account that you intended to leave for someone else, meanwhile triggering those unintended side effects and having to spend even more money just to cover the taxes.

There is a way to get rid of your RMD. If you do some thoughtful planning and take care of these pesky taxes ahead of time, you can fund an account that would allow you and your beneficiaries to withdraw contributions tax-free at any time. And once you've funded this strategy for at least five years, even the gains can be accessed without having to pay a penny in taxes.

Fast Fact: Once your RMD becomes due, for every dollar you fail to withdraw the IRS will charge a 50% penalty.[86]

Using the marginal income tax rates as a guide and working with an advisor, it's possible to pull out a strategic amount from your IRA every year while staying below your income threshold to fund a Roth. **Even if your income is higher than the maximum the IRS allows for regular Roth contributions, there is an IRS-sanctioned method for funding a Roth in retirement.** Withdrawals from your IRA will be taxed as income at your current rate, but because Roth withdrawals are not taxed, it can be a better deal for someone in a rising-tax environment.

---

[86] IRS, Correcting Required Minimum Distribution Failures, August 2021 https://www.irs.gov/retirement-plans/correcting-required-minimum-distribution-failures Accessed 10/25/2021.

When you convert to a Roth, you receive significant tax advantages:
- No RMDs.
- Tax-deferred growth.
- Tax-free gains.
- Tax-free income.
- Tax-free money to your beneficiaries.

All the money you put into a Roth can be taken out again without being reported on your 1040 tax form. Furthermore, when your account earns interest, you will not receive a 1099 form requiring you to report those gains, and even if your account doubles, you will have no RMD! All interest earned, whether it is from dividends or capitol gains, is distributed tax-free as long as the account has been open for at least five years.

In a rising-tax environment, this can be a real gift to both yourself and your beneficiaries because when you go to spend this money, nothing happens! You don't owe any income tax on the gains or on the money you take out, so the amount of your annual income as reported to the IRS and Social Security does not change. Your Social Security is not taxed at a higher rate, your marginal tax rate doesn't go up, and there is no change to the cost of your Medicare benefits.

Fast Fact: For 2022, you can contribute up to $7,000 to a Roth IRA if you are 50 or older and your modified AGI falls within the income limits.[87]

Prescription for Retirement Success: The goal when doing a Roth conversion is to pay the taxes owed on your IRA money while you are in the lowest possible income-tax bracket. So ask yourself if you would rather pay 23 cents on the dollar or 63 cents on the dollar? Be strategic. Even though you'll have to pay the taxes now, you'll be paying them at a known rate vs. an unknown rate that is likely to be much higher in the future. Act now before

---

[87] IRS, Retirement Topics – IRA Contribution Limits, Nov 2021 https://www.irs.gov/retirement-plans/plan-participant-employee/retirement-topics-ira-contribution-limits Accessed 3/4/2022.

rates change, and work with a financial advisor versed in tax efficiency who keeps up with the latest methods and rules.

CALL TO ACTION: Diversify your tax landscape

- ✔ Forecast your RMD to figure out whether the income will be usable or excess.
- ✔ Open up a Roth IRA and begin funding it to get the five-year clock ticking.
- ✔ Diversify your tax landscape so that you have optimum sources of tax-free and tax-advantaged retirement income.

FINAL THOUGHTS

"The great aim of education is not knowledge but action."

~ Herbert Spencer

Thank you for taking the time to make an investment in your fiscal health. It is my hope that you will use this knowledge to create a retirement that is filled with abundance for yourself and the people that you love.

I'd like to credit my mentor Scott Keffer who used to ask his clients at the end of a session to "do these five things." As a parting gift, I'd like to share with you the five things that I've adapted for my financial planning practice. I encourage you to put your new knowledge into action by doing the following:

Start today: Write out a to-do list, make a phone call, set an appointment with a professional. Take one step to improve your financial standing today.

Begin with what is most important to you: You don't have to follow the sequence outlined in this book. If there's a pressing concern on your mind, start there.

Hire a specialist: You've spent a lifetime accumulating wealth because you're good at your job. Let someone who is good at their job help maximize the opportunities and dodge the inherent pitfalls associated with your distribution years.

Create a comprehensive and coordinated plan: Because your withdrawals affect your taxes and income and peace of mind, get a plan that looks at the whole picture and includes everything: investments, taxes, Social Security, income, Medicare, RMD, and your hopes and dreams.

Nike: Just do it.

ABOUT THE AUTHOR

As the co-owner of Elite Income Advisors, Inc., Prashant R. Sabapathi is an investment advisor dedicated to helping business owners and individuals accumulate, protect, and pass on their wealth while minimizing tax liabilities over the course of their lifetimes. After getting into the financial services industry back in 2012, he saw the limitations of working as a captive agent for a corporate entity, and in 2014 he transitioned to becoming an independent advisor held to the fiduciary standard. He holds his Series 6, 63, and 65 licenses in addition to his life and health license in the state of Maryland. Using a client-centric approach, Prashant customizes each client's investment plan based on their specific financial objectives while implementing his philosophy that losses hurt more than gains help.

A recognized financial educator and retirement planner, Prashant was named to the Council of Financial Educators (COFE) and is a guest contributor on the nationally syndicated *Financial Safari* radio show and co-host on *Retire Smart Maryland* television. A lifelong Marylander, he grew up in Ellicott City in a family of doctors, attended McDonogh School for college prep, and graduated with a degree in economics from the University of Maryland, College Park.

As a musician who started playing piano at the age of four, Prashant has also developed his musical passion to master six instruments including guitar, mandolin, and electric violin. More recently, he was named to the Planned Giving Advisory Council for the Baltimore Symphony Orchestra. When not in the office, he can be found playing one of his six musical instruments, spending time with his fiancée, or enjoying the Maryland community with family and friends.

Glossary of Terms

ACCUMULATION PHASE – The financial phase during your working years when you are saving and growing your assets.

BUY-AND-HOLD – A passive investment strategy whereby market investments are bought and then held for a long period regardless of market fluctuations, so investors capture 100 percent of market gains and 100 percent of market loss.

COST-OF-LIVING ADJUSTMENT – Also known as COLA, these adjustments give claimants of Social Security a way to keep pace with inflation and the rising price of goods and services.

COMBINED INCOME – The IRS defines combined income as your adjusted gross income, plus tax-exempt interest, plus half of your Social Security benefits.

DELAYED RETIREMENT CREDITS (DRCs) – Credits used to increase the amount of your Social Security benefit during the period beginning with the month you achieve full retirement age and ending with the month you turn age 70.

DISTRIBUTION PHASE – The financial phase during your non-working years when you are spending the assets you saved.

FIDUCIARY – A professional who holds a legal or ethical relationship of trust to prudently take care of money or other assets for another person.

FULL RETIREMENT AGE (FRA) – Also known as normal retirement age, this is the age at which you become entitled to receive your full or unreduced retired worker benefit from Social Security.

INCOME ANNUITY – A flexible insurance tool that uses an indexing method to give you market-linked gains without direct exposure to market risk, with the option for income at some future date.

INCOME GAP – The difference between your retirement living expenses and the income from guaranteed sources such as pensions or Social Security.

INFLATION – The general rate at which the price of goods and services gradually rises.

IRMAA – An acronym for Medicare's income-related monthly adjustment amount, which can charge a higher premium for Medicare Part B and D for individuals with higher incomes.

PRINCIPAL – The base amount of money that you put into an investment.

PRIMARY INSURANCE AMOUNT (PIA) – The amount of money you will receive from Social Security if you file at your normal or full retirement age, rounded down to the next lower whole dollar amount.

REQUIRED MINIMUM DISTRIBUTION (RMD) – The minimum amount you must withdraw from qualified retirement accounts such as a traditional IRA by April 1 following the year you reach age 70½ or age 72.

ROTH IRA – Individual retirement arrangement made with income after the taxes have been paid where designated funds can grow tax-free with no taxes due on the interest earned if the rules for withdrawal are followed.

SSA – An acronym that stands for the Social Security Administration.

TRADITIONAL IRA – An individual retirement arrangement that provides a way to set aside money for retirement using contributions that are subtracted from your income (reducing the income taxes owed) and allowed to grow tax-free until the money is withdrawn, at which point taxes are owed on both the principal and interest earned.